# ENDORSEMENTS

Lana Vawser's *Woman of God, Fully Alive* is a life-changing call to embrace your divine identity and purpose. Through prophetic insight and wisdom, Lana empowers you to break free from fear, live boldly, and walk confidently in your God-given calling. I love Lana—she is a righteous encourager, anointed with the Holy Spirit. This book will awaken you to your true potential in Christ!

**Patricia King**
Christian Minister
Author, Media Host

This book truly is for every woman of God. Every woman who longs for the Lord and His genuine friendship—the kind of friendship that leads to life. Throughout the pages, I felt Lana giving me access to key after key for coming up higher in Him. For returning to our call as women to live ascended in intercession and our mothering. A needed word for us as mums! Lana's heart and revelation draw you in to reveal what it is to become transformed and redeemed from the inside out. This book is an invitation beckoning a generation of women to return to living out motherhood, kingdom purpose, and life, fully alive in our Savior.

**Bianca Serratore**
Founding Pastor of Fire Church Gold Coast and Arise Women Global

When reading through *Woman of God, Fully Alive*, I realized that this is a book that I could read on repeat, allowing the love of Jesus to wash over again and again. Lana speaks truths from the heart of the Father that will revive forgotten promises the Lord has spoken in past seasons and rekindle the fire of the kingdom calling on your life. This powerful book is full of encouragement and strategy to re-fix your gaze on Jesus, come up higher with Him, and walk boldly in the identity, authority, and kingdom plans that He has placed in you.

**Rebekah Bartels**
Mother, Worship Leader

In *Woman of God, Fully Alive*, Lana masterfully captures the Father's heart with profound grace and tenderness. Having witnessed these pages come to life during their creation, I can attest that her words create sacred pathways into deeper intimacy with God. Like a songbird's gentle call, this book beckons readers into the secret chambers of His presence, where His wings offer both shelter and rest.

This isn't merely a book to read once and set aside—it's a treasure you'll return to repeatedly, each time discovering new layers of His love. Through Lana's divinely inspired words, I found myself enveloped in His perfect security and unconditional acceptance. Her daily journeys into God's presence have carved out a beautiful road map for others to follow, inviting us all into a more profound and intimate relationship with the Lord.

Thank you, Lana, for showing us the way into these sacred spaces and teaching us how to dwell there.

**Roma Waterman**
Founder HeartSong Prophetic Alliance
Author, Teacher, Songwriter, Worship Leader

This book is a powerful invitation for every woman to step into her true identity in Christ—healed, whole, and unshakable. With deep insight and loving encouragement, Lana beckons women to embrace their God-given purpose and design with boldness and grace. She beautifully speaks to the heart of intimacy with Jesus and to experience the fullness of life that comes from a deep, abiding connection with Him. As you turn these pages, you will discover the transformative power of God's healing and restoration, wooing you to live whole and fully alive and to boldly speak His truth and declare His glory with unwavering confidence in these days ahead. It is my joy to recommend this powerful book from my beautiful friend, Lana.

**Natalie Fuller**

Author of Positioned for Purpose

www.nataliefuller.co

Authentic. Real. Raw. Pure. This is what you'll find in *Woman of God, Fully Alive*. Lana shares her personal journey of growing into a woman of God, fully alive. It's a powerful call to deeper intimacy—fixing our eyes on Jesus, sitting at His feet, and waiting on Him to move. Having journeyed closely with Lana for years as fellow mothers raising our children, I can testify that this book was birthed from personal encounter, healing, and transformation. Through every challenge, she has stood firm, watching God fight for her—and now, she shares this book with us.

*Woman of God, Fully Alive* is a timely call for women to arise, just as Deborah did—a mother.

**Kathryn Reed**

Mother, Worship Leader

*Woman of God, Fully Alive* is a sturdy dose of courage and fortitude, wrapped with practical application and encouragement. Lana Vawser skillfully teaches women what it looks like to navigate the challenges and warfare that comes to deter them from their destiny. This book not only equips women with strength and might in their own personal walk with Christ, it ministers deeply to the heart of the daughters of God where healing and encouragement is needed. *Woman of God, Fully Alive* is not just a book, it is a blueprint for this very hour. It is a clarion call to each woman in Christ to raise her head and to take her place in the world with confidence and strength, fully alive!

**Courtney Kueck**
Co-Host of Zion's Company of Women Podcast with Lana Vawser

*Woman of God, Fully Alive* is an outstanding piece from Lana Vawser, equipping God's daughters to rise boldly in their God-given design. Lana deeply carries the heart of the Father for women and the anointing on this book is like a balm of Gilead bringing comfort to the afflicted simultaneously injecting faith into the heart like a defibrillator bringing resurrection life. A Lana Vawser signature, intimacy with the Lord, is front and center equipping the heart to position for strategy, strength and henceforth victory. Her eloquent, single-hearted release of the word of the Lord to His daughters in this hour consequently imparts an "I won't take no for an answer" battle position. Ferocious in focus and ferocious in faith, this book will call forth the lioness out of every woman to be more than a conqueror through Christ who loves them.

**Dr Anita Alexander**
Prophetic Revivalist and Senior Leader, Golden City Church

Ah! "A woman of God who looks into God's eyes lives fully alive." What a beautiful truth! My dear friend Lana knows what it means to gaze into those beautiful eyes, and this book will inspire you to lift your head and be restored, strengthened, and loved by the affection that flows from His gaze.

The love of God is the foundation of our lives. To know this incomprehensible love through the power of His Spirit is the pursuit and focus of my life. As you read this beautiful book, I believe God will stir your spirit to fix your eyes on things above and to pray for a continual experience of His love that seeks to fill you up so that you can overflow it to the world around you!

**Katherine Ruonala**
Senior Leader, Glory City Church
Founder and Facilitator of the Australian Prophetic Council

It is an absolute honor to endorse this powerful book from a friend I value and respect so much, Lana Vawser. Lana carries a profound prophetic voice that is awakening, equipping, and calling this generation into deeper intimacy with Jesus—and the Lord has given her a word for His daughters.

*Woman of God, Fully Alive* is a call to every woman of God to arise, flourish, and step into her divine destiny by the power of God's Spirit. This book is an invitation to encounter Jesus, break free from limitations, and live in the fullness of who He created you to be. I wholeheartedly recommend it and celebrate the anointing Lana carries for this generation.

**Hayley Braun**
Overseer, Bethel School of Supernatural Ministry
Author of *Surrendered to the Holy Spirit*

# WOMAN OF GOD

## *Fully Alive*

Destiny Image Books by Lana Vawser

*A Time to Selah—God's Prophetic Invitation for You to Step Out of Crisis and Enter Into His Perfect Peace*

*I Hear the Lord Say "New Era"—Be Prepared, Positioned, and Propelled Into God's Prophetic Timeline*

*The Prophetic Voice of God: Learning to Recognize the Language of the Holy Spirit*

*Woman of God, Fully Alive—Your Prophetic Call to Hear from Heaven, Live Fearlessly, and Fulfill Your Divine Assignment*

*God Is Speaking—The Supernatural Christian (Audiobook)*

# WOMAN OF GOD *Fully Alive*

YOUR PROPHETIC CALL TO HEAR FROM HEAVEN, LIVE FEARLESSLY & FULFILL YOUR DIVINE ASSIGNMENT

LANA VAWSER

DESTINY IMAGE® PUBLISHERS, INC.
P.O. Box 310, Shippensburg, PA 17257-0310
*"Publishing cutting-edge prophetic resources to supernaturally empower the body of Christ"*

This book and all other Destiny Image and Destiny Image Fiction books are available at Christian bookstores and distributors worldwide.

For more information on foreign distributors, call 717-532-3040.
Reach us on the Internet: www.destinyimage.com.

ISBN 13 TP: 978-0-7684-7961-4
ISBN 13 eBook: 978-0-7684-7962-1
Hardcover: 979-8-8815-0578-3
Large Print: 979-8-8815-0579-0

For Worldwide Distribution, Printed in the U.S.A.

1 2 3 4 5 6 7 8 / 29 28 27 26 25

# CONTENTS

# INTRODUCTION

Woman of God, this is your time to thrive. This is your time to live *fully alive* in Christ. The Lord gave me this assignment to write this book, because I believe that it is His heart for you to discover more and more each day what it means for you to live as a *Woman of God, Fully Alive.*

As we journey together through the pages of this book, I believe that what you read is going to be a deep well of encounter, healing, awakening, permission to flourish and be yourself and arise and run into your destiny in unprecedented ways.

A mighty move of the Holy Spirit has begun on earth among His daughters as He leads us deeper and deeper into what it means to truly live the abundant life in Christ (John 10:10). I have encountered the Lord's heart over and over again the last number of years for His daughters to arise, be free in Christ, and be all He has created them to be. That time has arrived.

I hear the Spirit of God say, "*You shall go deeper into My heart and encounter Me in new, fresh and unprecedented ways*" and "*You shall ascend My mountain, you shall come up higher and grow in greater ways, what it means to be a woman who governs from her seated place with Me.*" As you read through these pages you will hear the sound of boldness and authority loudly in most chapters, because the Lord is raising up His daughters living fully alive in Him, in deep intimacy and a fresh boldness and a mighty ferocious awakening to their authority is happening, right now. An army of dangerously powerful daughters of God, living fully alive in Christ are arising on earth like *never* before.

I sit here writing this book as a woman who is deeply in love with Jesus and my greatest desire and pursuit in life is to know Him. I also sit here as a wife to an amazing man, Kevin, and I also sit here writing this book as a mother. A mother of four beautiful children—Elijah, Judah, Benjamin, and Isabella Joy. I have learned so much about living as a woman of God, fully alive and still on a journey, as I raise my children and I encounter His heart for me as His daughter and for His daughters all around the earth. He has "met me in the mothering," and I have learned so much about His unconditional love and delight in me as His daughter as I sit at His feet and I raise my children.

So let us start this journey of discovering together...

As I sit here beginning to write this book, I hear His whisper, "*Tell them, Lana, I am raising them up in this hour, stronger than ever before and that strength is found in Me and in deep dependency.*"

I believe God is raising up an army of women in this new era who are an unstoppable force. They are not an unstoppable force because of their own ability or their own strength, they are a company of women arising in strength from the place of deep intimacy with their King and deep dependency upon Him. They are arising with greater revelation and conviction of their oneness *in* and union *with* Christ. I hear His heart for you to *flourish* in this hour like you never have before. This is the time for you to be—in greater ways than you have ever experienced before—enjoying the abundant life He has created for you, living fully alive and being who He created you to be.

I hear the Lord saying: "*Their complete dependence upon Me is dangerous to the enemy.*"

And the words of Graham Cooke surround me: "Your intimacy with God is your greatest weapon."

So...

> *On your feet, Daughter of Zion! Be threshed of chaff, be refined of dross. I'm remaking you into a people invincible, into God's juggernaut to crush the godless peoples. You'll bring their plunder as holy offerings to God, their wealth to the Master of the earth* (Micah 4:13 MSG).

I hear the Lord saying:

> *Many of My daughters have been in a very intense battle and many of them for a very long time. They have been to the threshing floor and refined of dross, but in the battle they have faced, I have been birthing strength and courage within them like they have never known before. The strength of the wind of My Spirit is accelerating in intensity and My daughters are "getting up on their feet again." I have done a very deep work within them and their roots are going down deeper and deeper in dependency upon Me and founded in Me, the One who never changes.*
>
> *Within many ferocious battles My daughters have faced where the enemy has been roaring at them, in the fire, in the wrestle, in the intensity and onslaught, they have found Me, and they are finding the* **roar** *of My authority and victory in deeper ways, and* **now** *it is coming forth stronger than ever. They have discovered and will continue to discover the roar that I have placed within them. My roar over them is awakening them to their true identity. It's a dynamic deliverance. I am awakening them to My goodness and My destiny for their lives. The lies and captivity of the mind, heart, and soul are suddenly falling off. The chains that have held My daughters for years, the chains that have come through generations, are suddenly breaking off.*

> *I am raising up My daughters in unity, My daughters the juggernauts in Me. Unstoppable in Me! No longer held back, but empowered and strengthened and unstoppable, branded as* ***unstoppable*** *from the place of deep dependency. (Juggernaut: a huge, powerful and overwhelming force.)*
>
> *They are an army! My daughters are now rising up free from slavery and bondage that has held them. They are rising up to a new level of freedom that is already theirs. They are rising up and stepping into greater levels of healing that is already theirs. They are rising up awakened to My roar* ***in them*** *and* ***within*** *them and My roar* ***through*** *them. They are going into areas where the enemy has set up camp through their prayer, intercession, and assignments to release the roar of My rhema and decreeing that which I am speaking.*

Daughter of God, the time has arrived for you to flourish in who you are in Him in ways you've never imagined or dreamed. I have never been more convinced of the plans and purposes for His daughters on earth to arise and flourish in all they have been called to than I do right now. It is His heart for you to flourish in who He has created you to be and to flourish in all He has called you to.

For so long, so many daughters of God have felt so contained. So many women of God have felt anything but "fully alive," and the question is posed by many women, especially those who have walked and endured really hard seasons, some over the last few years and some for decades: "What does it even mean to live, fully alive?" And for some who have been in these seasons of life where they have felt plummeted and pummeled by the waves of life, especially in the last few years, one blow after another, that question is even louder, "What does it mean to live as a woman of God, fully alive? I don't even remember what it feels like when I'm thriving, I feel like I am living in a constant state of survival...."

Can I encourage you and remind you that our peace and joy and thriving come not from circumstance, but are founded in Him. Could it be that His definition of "thriving" is very different from ours at times? (I know at times for me, it certainly has been!)

I hear Psalm 1:2-3 over you:

> *But His delight is in the law of the Lord, and in His law he meditates day and night. He shall be like a tree planted by the rivers of water, that brings forth its fruit in its season, whose leaf shall not wither; and whatever he does shall prosper* (NKJV).

> *But they delight in the law of the Lord, meditating on it day and night. They are like trees planted along the riverbank, bearing fruit each season. Their leaves never wither, and they prosper in all they do* (NLT).

If you find yourself in that survival mode, that "barely making it through each day," can I encourage you, this is your defining moment. This is the season when the Lord is breathing resurrection life upon your heart. First and foremost, hear me daughter of God, woman of God, sister in Christ, He cares about your heart. He so intricately created you. He gave you the beautiful heart that you carry, and who you are is a dream birthed in His heart—He cares about you. He cares about you flourishing. He cares about you being fully alive, not for what you can do for Him, but because of who you are. You are His! You are His delight! You are the very theme of His song (Song of Songs 2:1-2). He is enthralled by *your* beauty (Psalm 45:11), and He is bringing you deeper into a divine dance of intimacy, wholeness, and life. His heart is for you to flourish and live fully alive in your divine dance of intimacy with Him.

**Knowing Him and being fully known by Him.**

This book is not a "how to" live fully alive, this book is a journey of discovery into the depths of who He is, the space of deep intimacy with your King, heart to heart entwined with your Beloved, moving, swaying, living, breathing, having your being in the divine dance of intimacy with Him.

This book is an invitation to *behold Him!* The pages of this book are filled with revelation, prophetic insight, encouragement, wisdom, strategy that all come from the divine dance with our Beloved Jesus. These pages are filled with insight into the fruit of *"in Him we live and move and have our being"* (Acts 17:28 NKJV).

To live fully alive, daughters of God, women of God, is not complicated. It's not a ten-step formula—to live fully alive is to *abide* (John 15) in Him, to *yield* to Him, to know Him, to let Him lead us in the beautiful divine dance of intimacy and be fully known by Him. To seek first His Kingdom and all else will be added unto us (Matthew 6:33 KJV).

Living fully alive, is to know Him deeply in deep intimacy, to *behold Him and then to become!*

Are you ready to dive deeper into the journey of beholding His beauty and beholding His Majesty and letting Him love you and behold your beauty? To deeply and truly know your King and His adoration, devotion, and love for you like never before? And to live even more deeply seen, known, and loved by Him?

This may be a courageous step to "Let Him," but this is the positioning, the invitation to living as a woman of God, fully alive. *"Let Him smother me with kisses—His Spirit-kiss divine. So kind are your caresses, I drink them in like the sweetest of wine!"* (Song of Songs 1:2 TPT).

As Brian Simmons writes in his book, *The Sacred Journey*[1]:

> To enter the doorway of Jesus' heart we must begin by saying, "Let Him." We only bring him a yielded heart and must "let him" do the rest. God's loving grace means that he will be enough for us. We can "let him" be everything to us. We don't begin by doing, but by yielding. The Word of God is the kiss from the mouth of our Beloved, breathing upon us the revelation of His love. The Shulamite doesn't ask him for power, position, or promotion, but for a kiss. Intimacy with Jesus Christ is more important than anything else he can give us. The word for "kisses" and the word for "take a drink of wine" is nearly the same. The implication, as seen by ancient expositors, is that God's lovers will be drunk with love, the intoxicating kisses of His mouth. The Hebrew word for "kiss" is *nashaq,* which can also mean "to equip" or "to arm" (for battle).

We need His kisses to become equipped warriors for Him.

Daughter of God, as we sit as His feet like Mary, yielded, adoring Him, letting Him love us and knowing Him in the place of deep intimacy, we are arising as warriors on earth, partnering with Him in what I believe is the greatest move of God among His daughters that we have ever seen. You are part of this mighty move. He is calling you. It's time to ascend. It's time to come up higher. It's time to dive deeper into His heart.

This, my dear sister in Christ, is where it begins, and where everything changes; there are deep hidden things that He has for you to search out in the place of deep intimacy with Him. They are hidden for you to find, in Him.

> *It is the glory of God to conceal a matter, but the glory of kings is to search out a matter* (Proverbs 25:2 NKJV).

# 1

# A WOMAN OF GOD WHO LOOKS INTO GOD'S EYES LIVES FULLY ALIVE

God's words surrounded me, "*A woman of God who looks into My eyes, lives fully alive,*"

Daughter of God, you were created to live eye to eye with Jesus. You were created to live locked-eyed with your King. Daughter of God, that is where you live, fully alive. You were not created to live distracted. I want you to hear that today, daughter of God, you were not created to live distracted. Your design is to live eye to eye with your King!

The enemy would like to keep us in the place of distraction, where things are constantly vying for our *attention* and our *affection,* but the place of our greatest focus is our beautiful Jesus. Our King. Our wonderful Jesus.

In His eyes, there is life. As you look at Him and lock eyes with Him, you find *all* you need; because as you look into His eyes, you see who He is and who you are. You live, fully alive.

> *[Looking away from all that will distract us and] focusing our eyes on Jesus, who is the Author and Perfecter of faith [the first incentive for our belief and the One who brings our faith*

> *to maturity], who for the joy [of accomplishing the goal] set before Him, endured the cross, disregarding the shame, and sat down at the right hand of the throne of God [revealing His deity, His authority, and the completion of His work]* (Hebrews 12:2 AMP).

> *We look away from the natural realm and we focus our attention and expectation onto Jesus who birthed faith within us and who leads us forward into faith's perfection. His example is this: Because His heart was focused on the joy of knowing that you would be his, he endured the agony of the cross and conquered its humiliation, and now sits exalted at the right hand of the throne of God!* (Hebrews 12:2 TPT)

As we look into His eyes, we see life. We see hope. We see peace. We see joy. We see strength. We see wisdom. We see abundant grace. We see love. We see the divine embrace of acceptance, forgiveness, righteousness. We see holiness. We see beauty. We see what is possible for those who believe. We see the Word. We see strategy. We see solution. We see eternity. We see faith.

Looking at Him, we are forever changed.

> *And we all, with unveiled face, beholding the glory of the Lord, are being transformed into the same image from one degree of glory to another. For this comes from the Lord who is the Spirit.* [So all of us who have had that veil removed can see and reflect the glory of the Lord] (2 Corinthians 3:18 ESV).

> *We can all draw close to him with the veil removed from our faces. And with no veil we all become like mirrors who*

> *brightly reflect the glory of the Lord Jesus. We are being transfigured into his very image as we move from one brighter level of glory to another. And this glorious transfiguration comes from the Lord, who is Spirit* (2 Corinthians 3:18 TPT).

I remember one of the first encounters I had as a 16-year-old girl. I had just come to know Jesus and I was interning at a local church as a children's pastor. This particular day we were running a school holiday program and I was part of the leadership team assigned to watch over the children as they played basketball.

I was sitting in the bleachers watching them play, when all of a sudden I was taken into a vision. Before my eyes I saw the same basketball stadium I was looking at, but all the lights were off. The stadium was so dark, when suddenly a spotlight came on and highlighted one corner of the room—and all of a sudden I saw Him, my Beloved. My Jesus! There He was, standing in a tuxedo smiling. Then suddenly, another spotlight came on and highlighted the other corner of the room directly diagonal to where the Lord was standing. And then I saw it. It was me. Standing there in the most beautiful white, sparkly wedding gown I had ever seen.

I remember in this vision that music started to play and Jesus started walking toward the center of the room. As He did, I began to walk toward Him to meet Him there. We met in the middle of the stadium and He put out His hands motioning to me to put my hands in His. I knew what was happening. He was inviting me to dance. So I placed my hands in His, and He smiled and said to me, "*Just look at Me. Keep your eyes on Me.*" We began to dance and I realized I didn't know the steps. Again He spoke, "*Just look at Me. Keep your eyes on Me.*" There was an invitation into deeper surrender that I was being invited into as I looked into His eyes. It was an invitation to let go, to let Him lead, and He would guide me.

So I did.

I focused in on His eyes, the beauty of His eyes that looked at me with such love, such delight, such adoration—and all of a sudden we were dancing the most beautiful waltz. As we danced there was such rest, such joy, such delight, such deep intimacy and connection as we moved and flowed and danced across the stadium floor. As we danced, I was surrounded by the sense of deep simplicity. I know that sounds almost contradictory but it was the deep place of Matthew 6:33 (paraphrased):

> *Seek first the Kingdom of God and all else will be added to you.*

And you know what? Nothing else mattered in that moment. I felt more alive than I had ever felt in that moment. I felt so secure, so safe, so deeply loved, so adored, so embraced, and *so led*. His love that tangibly engulfed me, saturated me, and overcame me brought a deep divine exhale of rest within my entire being—and that feeling of feeling fully alive shouted loudly to me, "*This is what you were created for!*" From that day, I knew that my focus in life was not to know how to "do everything right" or "follow the right formula or steps," I just had to stay deep in His embrace.

Intimacy. Abiding. Connected.

As we danced, I remember realizing that my chest was upon His chest and I was filled with the sense of our hearts being connected, our hearts were *as one*.

> *In Him we live and move and have our being...* (Acts 17:28 NKJV).

To live as a woman fully alive is to live as a woman, a daughter, who knows Him and her primary focus in life is to know Him deeply and to be a friend of God; then from that place, we make Him known.

I want you to think about something with me for a moment. We have beautiful Scriptures in the Word of God such as:

> Proverbs 8:34-35 (TPT): "*If you wait at wisdom's doorway, longing to hear a word for every day, joy will break forth within you as you listen for what I'll say. For the fountain of life pours into you every time that you find me, and this is the secret of growing in the delight and the favour of the Lord.*"

> Matthew 4:4 (NKJV): "*But He answered and said, 'It is written, "Man shall not live by bread alone, but by every word that proceeds from the mouth of God."'*"

Every day, you, daughter of God, and I wake up and look up, behold His beauty, look into His eyes and hear from the One who created the heavens and the earth. The One who existed and is before all things, and in Him all things hold together (Colossians 1:17), the Almighty One, and He seeks to know you. He invites you and I daily into this place of listening and lingering before Him to hear, perceive, and receive what is on His heart and to feast upon His Word and His rhema. This perfect, beautiful One who invites us to come and sit at the table of intimacy with Him daily and dine with Him. The One whose Word never returns void (Isaiah 55:11) and the One who alone holds the words of eternal life (John 6:68), in *Him* there is life.

Every day as you lean in and listen, as you live at His feet as Mary did absorbing all that He is speaking to you (Luke 10:39), His nature, His heart, His presence, His Word, His whispers bring us deeper and deeper into life. True life that never changes, remains the same.

Always consistent, always faithful, always loving, always steadfast, always true.

What does John 10:10 (AMP) say?

> *The thief comes only in order to steal and kill and destroy. I came that they may have and enjoy **life,** and have it in abundance [to the full, till it overflows].*

In the glorious gift given to us of Christ laying down His life for us, His shed blood, His broken body, His resurrection, we find the remission of sin, forgiveness, righteousness, and *eternal life!* Forever united with Him for all eternity! Hallelujah!

The more we know Him, the more we see Him, the more we lock eyes with Him and look not away, the more and more we find life in Him. It's gloriously, deeply simple. To live fully alive is to live in Him and to know Him, and day by day His Word and whispers to you by His Spirit compel you and causes you to live *fully alive* in the abundant life that He has purchased for you, as His Words of life bring you into deeper revelation of eternal life and life in Him (John 6:68-69).

In this hour when there is so much noise and chaos on earth, so much distraction, so much vying for your focus, so much trying to steal life from you, contain you and cage you, the Father is drawing you deeper into His heart and deeper intimacy and further into the revelation of your identity, causing you to arise and shine in who He has created you to be in greater ways than you have ever known.

He is wooing you with His voice. He is calling you with His heart, "Come deeper, come deeper still."

Daughter of God, in these days, these very days that we are now living in, you are being called. You are being called to arise and shine, and it's time for you to step deeper and further into your destiny of knowing Him and fulfilling your assignment. No more hiding, no more shying away. No more wallflowers.

It's time for you to understand and walk in what it means to be a woman of God who lives fully alive.

This isn't just a new chapter for you.

It's a new era.

The enemy may have done all he can to fight for your focus, but the wooing of the heart of Christ for you is wooing you deeper into His gaze; and as you behold His beauty more and more, you are arising and becoming more of a woman who lives *fully alive.*

And trust me, daughter of God, that scares the enemy and he is going to be sorry he ever messed with you.

The fire in the eyes of Jesus (Revelation 19:12) is inviting you to be lock-eyed with Him afresh.

Get ready to be conquered afresh by the fire in His eyes.

# 2

# AS YOU BEHOLD, YOU BECOME

I believe there is a call from the Lord in this hour to "Behold Him" with greater ferocity and intentionality of focus. Where there has been such an intensity in this season that has attempted to distract God's people and cause them to feel trapped and "under" circumstances, opposition, trials, grief, pain, loss, and the effect of the seasons they have walked, God is calling His people up higher, into the place of beholding Him in greater ways.

How often have you felt like circumstances, life, the enemy, your own thoughts, have become really loud? Like all of a sudden the volume on these things has increased dramatically and then you have that volume increasing from so many different areas in your life. One minute you're battling the voice of insecurity or comparison speaking loudly to you, the next there is such an onslaught of confusion or heaviness accompanied with such intense accusation from the enemy; and while you're standing against that, life and circumstances are shouting *louder*. What can happen? Swirl can happen. We can end up feeling like we're living in a perpetual state of being spun around and around in a washing machine, desperately hoping it will stop so we can regain our balance and take a breather.

Daughter of God, woman of God, you were not created to live "waiting" for the storm to settle down so you can breathe. That is not your portion. You were created to live above the storm. You were created to be one who can stand strong in the storm and the swirl, not because of your own strength, but because of *whose* you are and who *He* is inside you. You were created to live victorious amid the swirl rather than the swirl of life dictating and governing you. You are created as a powerful woman of God, with the authority of Christ and the ability to walk in supernatural peace and joy and freedom, despite your circumstances.

Yet, the enemy fights so hard to cause you to bow under the swirl. You were created, daughter of God, to live above the swirls of life and to stay in a place of secure faith, peace, and hope no matter what, because you live and move and have your being (Acts 17:28) in the One who never changes (Hebrews 13:8). Everything you need for life and godliness is found in Jesus Christ.

> *Grace and peace be yours in abundance through the knowledge of God and of Jesus our Lord. His divine power has given us everything we need for a godly life through our knowledge of him who called us by his own glory and goodness* (2 Peter 1:2-3 NIV).

God has given us in Him, all that we need. We have everything. We are prepared, we are armed, we are *already* victorious in Christ. It has been given to us through knowing Him.

Precious sister in Christ, can you see how God has equipped you in Christ to live fully alive? Your circumstances are not your source of living fully alive. (Thank God!) Jesus is your Source! In Him is abundant life, and all you need has been given to you that pertains to life and godliness; so your job and mine is to lean into, access, and walk in, by faith, what has already been given to us. You were created to live, fully alive.

It's the call to ascend. It is the call to come up higher, and it isn't a place where you're "finally getting to ascend," it's where you are already seated and where you were created to live from.

> *Even when we were dead in trespasses,* [God] *made us alive together with Christ—by grace you have been saved—and raised us up with him and seated us with him in the heavenly places in Christ Jesus* (Ephesians 2:5-6 ESV).

I want you to understand this, this is where you were created to live. The enemy has lied to so many daughters of God with accusations such as, "This situation is never going to change," "You're never going to change," "This is just your lot in life." The barrage of accusations, intimidation, and onslaught of the enemy is aimed to weary many daughters of God and has caused many to feel like they are not living a life fully alive, but are instead living a life just trying to survive. That's not your lot, that's not your portion, that's not your inheritance in Christ.

You are called, daughter of God, woman of God, to live as *more* than a conqueror (Romans 8:37). You are called to *live* the ascended life. You are not called to "visit" the heavenly place and occasionally "visit" your seated place in Heaven, you *are already* seated in heavenly places with Christ Jesus. It's already done. Your positional inheritance is fixed by the death and resurrection of our beautiful King Jesus.

There has been such an onslaught and torment and attack of the mind against many daughters of God, because the Lord is raising up His daughters in this hour carrying divine intel, supernatural intelligence, wisdom, and strategy in ways we have never seen before.

The Lord is releasing His fire upon the eyes of His daughters in this hour to increase spiritual sight and divine insight as we lean in and listen to what the Spirit of God is saying. There is a sharpening of vision taking place, there's a deeper place of revelation to *see and discern* what the Lord is saying and what He is doing in this hour as we seek His heart and truly dive deep into the Word of God and knowing the Word of God.

There has been such an attack over the sight of many daughters in this hour. The confusion, the lack of clarity that has come suddenly against many daughters, the vision that has been stolen and broken down in the lives of many daughters, the enemy has been not only after the voice of the daughters in this hour, but also the sight of the daughters of God in this hour. I believe there is a mighty increase of insight being released to women in this hour to discern, perceive, and release what God is saying and what He is doing.

This attack against vision and against spiritual sight and divine insight being released to His daughters in this hour, is being broken off in this hour. As hard as the attack has come against many daughters of God in this hour to steal vision and divine sight through confusion, discouragement, despair, hopelessness, witchcraft attacks or fear, it's time for the daughters of God to arise and push back against the enemy and cry out to see Him and see what He is speaking and releasing with greater ferocity. The Spirit of God is stirring the cry within many hearts, the desperate cry to know Him and to see as He sees. This is the hour to purchase eye salve (Revelation 3:18-22) like never before. It's the hour to arise and ferociously reject all attacks of the enemy against your sight and your vision.

*Lord, come and wash our eyes, wash our eyes from anything that has hindered our vision. Wash our eyes, Lord, and let us see You and what You are speaking and releasing clearer than ever. Come, Lord, wash our eyes!*

It is time for the daughters of God to see clearer than they have ever seen. The Lord is severing the fog over the eyes of His daughters and raising them up in this hour with a supernatural vision to see further and deeper into the heavenly mysteries and divine strategies and solutions of the Lord. The Lord is raising up His daughters with crowns of wisdom in this hour that have been placed on their heads, as they have been sitting at the feet of Jesus, adoring Him, treasuring His wisdom and words and ministering unto Him.

## Behold!

I remember His whisper so clearly to me one day as I sat leaning in and listening to His heart with coffee in hand, and He said, *"As you behold, you become."*

I remember the sense of the Lord's encouragement to me so strongly, *"There is a battle over your* ***beholding, so behold!"***

I knew in that moment that the Lord was calling His daughters to make the decision to *behold* Him, over and over and over again. It was not a "religious striving" or "human effort," it was a greater call to attention that flowed from the place of affection and adoration of Him.

I saw a resolve that He was breathing into His daughters, an empowering strength that says, "I am going to stand against this. If there's a battle over my beholding, to try to get my eyes off of Him and onto beholding everything else, then I am going to even more intentionally *behold Him." It* was a divine defiance that declared, "I will *not* align with the enemy and his attempts to distract and derail"—and a holy ferocious focus of heart intent, "I will not take My eyes off You, God. Holy Spirit, strengthen Me to keep my focus upon You and Your gaze."

The Lord spoke to me again: *"Lovers don't look away."*

You know that giddy love? When you're so deeply in love with someone, you can't stop looking at them? The Lord spoke to me that many daughters have experienced their burning, giddy, first-love fire for Jesus being dampened or squashed by the intensity of battle. If you find yourself in this place, I have encouragement for you.

Your heart cries out, *"Lord, cause my heart to burn for You again,"* and as you behold Him in His beauty, the unveiling of His nature and His majesty, His goodness and His glory is going to usher you deeply into the place of the re-introduction to that first-love fire. This isn't a place of human striving, it is the Lord's heart to restore that first-love fire within your heart again. He is going to conquer you with His love, again and again. Over and over as you behold Him.

He is coming after you in relentless pursuit to bathe your heart and saturate your entire being in His love again, a fresh baptism of fire that will wash and burn off all the weariness, battle exhaustion, and things that have dampened that fire and all the things that have tried to push you into "religious works" to try to "do do do." He is bringing you deeper into the place of rest in His love and the adoration of His nature. The Lord is removing the clutter. He is restoring simplicity in the first-love fire and walking in the garden with Him in flourishing intimacy, rather than the dry, barren wastelands that you may feel you have been walking in. The Lord is leading you deeply into the song of His heart in the song of songs to reawaken you to His love and adoration *of you!*

There is so much battle over your beholding. For what you behold is what you become, and the enemy knows this. The Lord is calling His daughters higher into the place of beholding His beauty:

> *Here's the one thing I crave from Yahweh, the one thing I seek above all else: I want to live with him every moment in his house, beholding the marvelous beauty of Yahweh, filled with awe, delighting in his glory and grace...* (Psalm 27:4 TPT).

In that place there is a glorious birthing, awakening, and transformation that happens, to realign you with who you are created and called to be and further into who He has made you to be. The chains fall off. The comparison melts away. The fear breaks. The intimidation flees. Because as you look at Him, as you behold His beauty, things become clear. As you behold Him and you hear Him speak, you see Him afresh, you see how you were created in His image. As you behold His beauty, His love, His goodness, and His presence, His power conquers you again and again and again. As you behold Him, the revelation of *who* His, and *seeing* who He is, changes *everything*.

I hear the Lord saying, "*A woman of God living fully alive, is one who looks again and again and again and again.*"

When the Lord spoke these words, I saw women all around the earth, with eyes on Jesus, beholding His beauty; and as they leaned in and looked deeper and deeper into who He is, their hearts were filled with the expectancy and childlike wonder "to look again and again and again," seeking Him deeper every day. To be ones who are living awakened to the invitation to see Him afresh and discover a new part of Him and His nature every day in their beholding of Him.

## Look Again

When the enemy has come against many daughters of God, he loudly proclaims: "Look again at your circumstances," "Look again at how you feel," "Look again at what you've lost," "Look at what's broken," "Look at how broken you feel," "Look at what you've done," "Look at what you've become," "Look at what hasn't happened," "Look at what has happened," and over and over again. The enemy has come against many daughters to cause them to "Look again" to the temporal realm, the natural realm, the natural way of thinking.

Yet the Lord is calling His daughters to "come up higher and behold—look again and again and again at Me and be left in the awe of My love for you."

I heard the Lord say:

> *The enemy has come with the lure for My daughters to "look again" and "look again," and the temptation of the flesh has yelled "look again" to all that is not in alignment with what I am speaking and what My heart is saying. The enemy says, "look again" at the natural realm that brings such weariness. But I am raising up My daughters to "look again and again and again at* **Me** *to see another part of My heart every day," and they are left in* **wonder.** *They live a life of keeping their eyes firmly fixed on Me, and whatever the circumstance, they look again at what I am speaking and what I am revealing, rather than looking again at the natural realm.*

I heard the Lord say: "*As you behold, I am realigning.*"

The Lord is bringing divine order into the lives of His daughters in such a beautiful, tangible, and powerful way. He is bringing what has been out of alignment, into His perfect alignment. He is bringing what was out of order, into divine order. Where our focus, our vision, our sight has been skewed, attacked, or hindered, the Lord is bringing a realignment of vision. I hear the Lord say where you have "seen" things in your life that have been out of order, you are going to "see" the divine order of the Lord come to pass in your life in His mighty realignments, as you behold Him. Keep your eyes on Him.

> *Looking away [from all that will distract] to Jesus, Who is the Leader and the Source of our faith [giving the first incentive for our belief] and is also its Finisher [bringing it to mature and perfection]...* (Hebrews 12:2 AMPC).

There is divine clarity that the Lord is releasing as you behold Him, a clarity that replaces confusion. As you behold Him and meet with Him in the Word, a mighty move of His Spirit removes the cloud of confusion you may have felt like you have been living under for so long and you will come up higher and higher in your sight, to see as He sees and see the great and mighty things that He has to show you (Jeremiah 33:3; Revelation 4:1).

I believe, to live as a woman of God, fully alive, is to live as a woman fully aligned. Focused upon Jesus, eyes fixed on Him. It's not a striving or a struggle, it's the joy in the divine dance of intimacy of letting Him lead and guide you.

One of my favorite hymns, "Turn Your Eyes Upon Jesus" by Helen H. Lemmel (1922), was inspired by a song and poem titled "Focussed" written by Lilias Trotter (1853-1928) that I came across on Jennifer Miskov's blog where it says:

> Lilias Trotter (1853-1928) originally from London, England was an anointed artist who had a potential career path direction if she chose to take it. Famous art critics saw her early work and were even willing to invest in her training because of the huge potential they saw in her as an artist. While she loved art, she also felt a calling from God to reach the lost. She began engaging in this call while in London by going out into the streets in the late hours of the night by herself to reach and rescue prostitutes off of the streets. She also felt a calling to share Jesus with the unreached people groups in Algeria in Northern Africa. Responding to this calling would come at a great cost as it would require her to lay down her budding career as an artist. As she responded to this call, no mission agencies would send her there or support her mission. Not deterred, she decided to still follow the call of God to Africa and go by herself. She lived among the nationals in the hiddenness of the desert there for forty years. There, in the desert, Trotter knew what it was like to be stripped from every distraction to focus upon the face of Jesus. She had laid her life down for that one purpose. While

> there, she wrote the poem that later inspired the song "Turn Your Eyes Upon Jesus." (jenmiskov.com)

I want to encourage you to slowly walk through this poem and song, and allow it to speak to you. Allow the Holy Spirit to minister to you, because God is calling us as His daughters to a ferocious focus upon beholding Him, where all else fades away.

This is where we come, fully alive!

"Focussed: A Story and a Song" by Lilias Trotter

> It was in a little wood in early morning. The sun was climbing behind a steep cliff in the east, and its light was flooding nearer and nearer and then making pools among the trees. Suddenly, from a dark corner of purple brown stems and tawny moss, there shone out a great golden star. It was just a dandelion, and half withered—but it was full face to the sun, and had caught into its heart all the glory it could hold, and was shining so radiantly that the dew that lay on it still made a perfect aureole round its head. And it seemed to talk, standing there—to talk about the possibility of making the very best of these lives of ours.
>
> For if the Sun of Righteousness has risen upon our hearts, there is an ocean of grace and love and power lying all around us, an ocean to which all earthly light is but a drop, and it is ready to transfigure us, as the sunshine transfigured the dandelion, and on the same condition—that we stand full face to God.
>
> Gathered up, focussed lives, intent on one aim—Christ—these are the lives on which God can concentrate blessedness. It is "all for all" by a law as unvarying as any law that governs the material universe.
>
> We see the principle shadowed in the trend of science; the telephone and the wireless in the realm of sound, the use

of radium and the ultra violet rays in the realm of light. All these work by gathering into focus currents and waves that, dispersed, cannot serve us. In every branch of learning and workmanship the tendency of these days is to specialize—to take up one point and follow it to the uttermost.

And Satan knows well the power of concentration, if a soul is likely to get under the sway of the inspiration, "this one thing I do," he will turn all his energies to bring in side-interests that will shatter the gathering intensity.

And they lie all around, these interests. Never has it been so easy to live in half a dozen good harmless worlds at once—art, music, social science, games, motoring, the following of some profession, and so on. And between them we run the risk of drifting about, the "good" hiding the "best" even more effectually than it could be hidden by downright frivolity with its smothered heart-ache at its own emptiness.

It is easy to find out whether our lives are focused, and if so, where the focus lies. Where do our thoughts settle when consciousness comes back in the morning? Where do they swing back when the pressure is off during the day? Does this test not give the clue? Then dare to have it out with God—and after all, that is the shortest way. Dare to lay bare your whole life and being before Him, and ask Him to show you whether or not all is focussed on Christ and His glory. Dare to face the fact that unfocussed good and useful as it may seem, it will prove to have failed of its purpose.

What does this focussing mean? Study the matter and you will see that it means two things—gathering in all that can be gathered, and letting the rest drop. The working of any lens—microscope, telescope, camera—will show you this. The lens of your own eye, in the room where you are sitting, as clearly as any other. Look at the window bars, and the beyond is only a shadow; look through at the distance, and it is the bars that turn into ghosts. You have to choose which you will fix your gaze upon and let the other go.

Are we ready for a cleavage to be wrought through the whole range of our lives, like the division long ago at the taking of Jericho, the division between things that could be passed through the fire of consecration into "the treasury of the Lord," and the things that, unable to "bide the fire," must be destroyed? All aims, all ambitions, all desires, all pursuits—shall we dare to drop them if they cannot be gathered sharply and clearly into the focus of "this one thing I do"?

Will it not make life narrow, this focusing? In a sense, it will—just as the mountain path grows narrower, for it matters more and more, the higher we go, where we set our feet—but there is always, as it narrows, a wider and wider outlook and purer, clearer air. Narrow as Christ's life was narrow, this is our aim; narrow as regards self-seeking, broad as the love of God to all around. Is there anything to fear in that?

And in the narrowing and focussing, the channel will be prepared for God's power—like the stream hemmed between the rockbeds, that wells up in a spring—like the burning glass that gathers the rays into an intensity that will kindle fire. It is worth while to let God see what He can do with these lives of ours, when "to live is Christ."

How do we bring things to a focus in the world of optics? Not by looking at the things to be dropped, but by looking at the one point that is to be brought out.

Turn full your soul's vision to Jesus, and look and look at Him, and a strange dimness will come over all that is apart from Him, and the Divine "attrait" by which God's saints are made, even in this 20th century, will lay hold of you. For "He is worthy" to have all there is to be had in the heart that He has died to win.[2]

# 3

# AN INVITATION INTO REVELATION THAT BRINGS WHOLENESS

I remember the place where I was sitting in my home as I sat in the middle of a time when I felt the weight of pain, grief, trauma, and loss from a long, long season. I remember sitting in that room feeling so overwhelmed by the pain of such a hard, long journey, where holding onto belief and faith in what God had spoken had only seemingly met me with much pain, grief, and loss. It was one of those moments when the process felt just too much. Hopelessness and despair were fighting hard to be the loudest voices in my heart and in my mind and again the reality of Psalm 46:1:

> *God is our refuge and strength, always ready to help in times of trouble* (NLT).
>
> *God, you're such a safe and powerful place to find refuge! You're a proven help in time of trouble—more than enough and always available whenever I need you* (TPT).

I really needed Him. I felt so far from "woman of God, fully alive," but the truth was that He was leading me farther into the wholeness that was already mine in Christ, He was growing me up into wholeness.

So as I sat there, knowing He was present to help me in every need, I cried out.

That's when He came and met me.

I was taken into an encounter where Jesus grabbed my hand and stood me at the doorway of a house. I knew that somehow this house represented me or my life. He began to walk me into some of the rooms in this house. Some were sparkling golden and full of light, but then He took me into a few rooms and I was shocked with what I saw. The walls were black. That's right, black! I know enough about seeing in the spirit to know that's not a good thing. But what happened next, was just like Jesus.

He spoke these words:

*"I am going to clean and transform every room and every part."* Then He walked up to the walls that were black and with His hand He began to wipe the black off and what was revealed was beautiful, sparkling gold walls. One by one He walked to each wall and with a swipe of His hand, He removed the black.

Instantly I knew that these were parts of my heart that had faced grief, trauma, pain, disappointment, and loss in that season, but they were not my story and they were not who I was. They were not my inheritance, nor my design. As I watched Jesus wipe away that black stain and the gold, sparkling walls were revealed, I knew in my spirit that my *experience* had not marred the original design. The original design of my identity had not been marred or affected by what I had experienced or walked through. My identity and my positional inheritance in my identity was secure because of what Christ did for me. What I had walked and was walking was not who I was, and that voice did not have the right to be the loudest voice in my heart and in my life. His voice, His truth, and His reality was to be the loudest voice in my heart and mind.

Because I am a woman, created to live *fully alive,* I am going to *align* with what He is speaking over me and over my identity in His original design of who I am. In our journey of arising as women of God *fully alive,* it is imperative that we *align* with our original design.

The words He spoke: *"There is an invitation into revelation that brings wholeness."* It was the reality that one word out of His mouth changes everything. It was the truth and reality that transformation happens when we see Him; transformation happens when He speaks.

So many verses in the Word fill my heart and mind about the power of His voice. His voice is like thunder (Ezekiel 3:12), His voice is like a hammer (Jeremiah 23:29), His voice creates (Genesis 1:1,3,6,9,11,20...) and we experience this transformation because of *who* is speaking. Transformation happens when Jesus walks in the room; when He steps in, everything changes. When He walks into those rooms of our hearts that are holding pain, trauma, grief, or loss, His presence, His love and His Word, bring healing. He speaks a better word.

**Revelation reveals and heals.**

I heard the Lord say: *"I am flipping the script in your life."*

I looked up the definition of "to flip the script" and found: "To reverse the usual or existing positions in a situation and do something unexpected or revolutionary" (Google) and "To turn the tables on" (thefreedictionary.com).

I believe that today the Lord is going to change the narrative that has been speaking opposite to what the Lord says about you and the truths of His Word and bring you into greater wholeness that is already yours in Christ as you go deeper into the discovery of His narrative and His truth and rhema over your life.

Song of Songs 1:5 (TPT) says:

*The Shulamite: "Jerusalem maidens, in this twilight darkness,*
*I know I am so unworthy—so in need."*

> *The Shepherd-King: "Yet you are so lovely!"*
>
> *The Shulamite: "I feel as dark and dry as the desert tents of the wandering nomads."*
>
> *The Shepherd King: "Yet you are so lovely—like the fine linen tapestry hanging in the Holy Place."*

Look at this conversation here between the Shulamite woman and the Shepherd King. She speaks of feeling so unworthy and so in need; yet how does the Shepherd-King respond? He responds with love and her true identity.

Brian Simmons, in his book *The Sacred Journey,* calls it "Abba's anyway love," and I love that phrase because in the process of growing up into wholeness and maturity, Abba Father does not leave us where we are. He does not point out all our flaws and see what is wrong with us. No. He calls us up and into our true identity in Christ, and how He sees us.

> Abba's "anyway love" is here. He can say, "Yes, I know and you know that sin has brought shame, but I love you anyway. Your longings for Me make you lovely. With a willing spirit you will go on to a mature bridal love. (*The Sacred Journey,* p. 28)

As I read this passage, I continued to stop at the word *yet.* The Lord continued to highlight this word to me, so again being the lover of words that I am, I went to the dictionary. Yet: "An expression used to say that something has not happened up to now" (Google).

This struck me, because as I look at the Shulamite in this conversation with the Shepherd-King that word *yet,* speaks to me of transformation. This is a moment of transformation for her, and where the journey into "growing up into wholeness" begins. That word *yet* is a pivotal place for her encounter with the Shepherd-King, that "anyway love" of Abba Father that draws her deeper into wholeness, flourishing, and maturity of her original design.

The Lord is not making changes to you and who He created you to be in your original design, He is loving you to life, growing you up into wholeness, freeing you, delivering you, and healing you of what has attempted to hide the beauty of you. The beauty of who He created you to be.

We watch the journey of the Shulamite into wholeness that comes as we are—to borrow Brian Simmon's phrase from *The Sacred Journey*—***"conquered by love."*** We watch as the Shulamite moves into healing into freedom into maturity and wholeness. How? Through His love and His Words of truth spoken over her. She is conquered and made whole in the revelation of His love and the revelation of His truth spoken over her and into her.

Every time He speaks over her it is an *"invitation into revelation that brings wholeness."*

> **The divine exchange table—He was broken and wounded so we could be made whole.**
>
> *But He was wounded for our transgressions, He was crushed for our wickedness [our sin, our injustice, our wrongdoing]; the punishment [required] for our well-being fell on Him, and by His stripes (wounds) we are healed* (Isaiah 53:5 AMP).

I remember a number of years ago, I was going through an intense journey of healing and deliverance from the lies of the enemy over who I was and my identity in Christ. I remember there were so many lies that I believed about who I was that I didn't even know where to begin in my repentance and renewing my mind. I sat on my office floor and I cried out to Him, "Lord, I need to know Your truth. I know that one word out of Your mouth changes everything." Then, our ever-present help in time of need, our beautiful Jesus drew me into an encounter that marked me for life. It was the vision that changed my life.

## The Vision That Changed My Life

I remember seeing Jesus kneeling over a broken tree stump. I looked at His hands and they were tied with rope. I looked at His head and there was a crown of thorns upon it. Behind Him I saw a man standing there dressed like a Roman centurion. I noticed in the hands of this Roman centurion was what looked like a whip. As I stood there I noticed the enemy was standing to the left of Jesus and he was looking at me and started to accuse me, he was accusing me of things in my past, he was saying, "This is who you are." His accusation of me was relentless. But what changed my life was this.

*Each time* the enemy accused me, the man on the left with the whip whipped Jesus across the back, and Jesus cried out in pain—then He decreed the truth and the truth of who I am and His great love for me and what He had called me to. I knew in that moment in the very core of my being that Jesus had taken it all—my sin, all of it, and that I stand in Him righteous and free and forgiven by the blood of Jesus. He took all those accusations upon Himself so I could be whole and healed. It was His voice, the voice of truth and the power of His voice and His love that healed and transformed me.

That vision was an invitation into the revelation that ushered me into wholeness. The wholeness in Christ that is my positional inheritance because of what He purchased for me.

That revelation shifted my entire life. The enemy was attempting to "bait me into belief of his accusations and what he was speaking over me," but the Lord's heart was to *build me into belief* in who *He* says I am and that I am *already whole* in Christ because He was crushed for my sin, and He was wounded so I could *be whole.*

Our perspective and belief about wholeness will shape how we walk the journey and process into greater wholeness, every day of our lives. It's a journey, and we cannot live below the positional inheritance of wholeness we have been given in Christ by allowing the enemy to "bait us into belief of his accusations." We must arise as daughters of God who live by every word that flows out of His mouth (Matthew 4:4) and what He speaks over us, being the loudest voice.

Because we are *already* whole in Christ, each day we are *growing up into wholeness.* As I walk the journey further into wholeness every day, my perspective matters. I need to live *from* the place of revelation that I am *already whole,* not "trying to *be* whole." A rest is found in the revelation of my positional inheritance of wholeness that *He* purchased for me; as I align with this truth, I walk in faith and victory. Perspective matters. Faith in what He speaks, matters.

I remember a time when I was battling with intense heaviness, accusation, and heavy discouragement, so I went to the Lord for help. The Lord spoke to me in that moment and said to me, "Lana, you actually believe the lies that the enemy has accused you of." Ouch! I had given the enemy legal right and a landing pad through my belief and agreement. I was quick to repent and in that moment there was another level of "invitation into revelation that brings wholeness" that I was met with. This time it was the revelation that I had aligned with lies about who I am, and that very acknowledgement brought a shift and realignment and made room for greater wholeness in me as a fire of faith was ignited afresh in me to not give the enemy any of my faith, but step further into who He says that I am. I had settled for lies without even realizing it, and the Lord, shining His truth on this, exposed it and brought me deeper into the alignment of truth. I had to renew my mind (Romans 12:2).

God's heart for me was to "build me into belief" and that is His heart for you, whole woman. To build you into belief, His belief of you. His heart for you is to "conquer you with love" over and over and over again, that like the Shulamite woman. Wherever you find yourself on your journey with your Beloved, whether you feel like you are hiding behind walls of fear, compromise or shame, or you are flourishing, can I say that whichever "camp" we find ourselves in, ***we are all growing up into wholeness.***

You, whole woman, are growing up into the wholeness that is already yours in Christ. You are already whole and growing up into it. There is *always* more on this beautiful, sometimes painful, messy yet incredible journey into wholeness as the invitation into revelation of who He is and what He speaks over you, brings wholeness.

> **This invitation into revelation that brings wholeness requires a response.**

Inactivity ensures you *remain* where you are; *intentionality* ensures you *move, grow, and transform.*

This journey of wholeness requires intentionality. What does that intentionality look like?

> *My son, pay attention to my words and be willing to learn; open your ears to my sayings. Do not let them escape from your sights; keep them in the center of your heart. For they are life to those who find them, and healing and health to all flesh. Watch over your heart with all diligence, for from it flow the springs of life* (Proverbs 4:20-23 AMP).

> *So* ***above all****, guard the affections of your heart, for they affect all that you are. Pay attention to the welfare of your innermost being, for from there flows the wellspring of life* (Proverbs 4:23 TPT).

Brian Simmons, in *The Passion Translation* footnotes on Proverbs 4:23, says:

> The Hebrew word *levav* is the most common word for "heart." It includes our thoughts, our wills, our discernment, and our affections. Although most translations have "the issues of life," the Hebrew word *casa* is actually "seasons," especially springtime. Out of your heart flow the seasons of life. It is our hearts, not our ages or circumstances, that shape the seasons of our lives. If our hearts are tender to God, we can live in perpetual springtime.

This is a powerful revelation. This is another moment of the invitation into revelation that brings wholeness. If I truly get this, this transforms how I live and highlights a very important priority. I am to guard the affections of my heart.

Joyce Meyer defines *to guard* as: "To be alert, to be conscious and aware of my thoughts and attitudes and not let the enemy or anything else poison my heart with lies and deceits. Many wrong and vicious thought patterns and attitudes are built up in us 'little by little.' We must remember that satan is very patient, and he is relentless, so we must be even more relentless than he is. Guard your heart with all diligence."

See the words: "We must be even more relentless than he is."

We are the watchman over our hearts. We are the gatekeepers over our hearts. If we are going to arise in this hour as whole women and women who are living fully alive, we must be ones who live with intentionality. We must be ones who live with intentionality over our hearts and not allow the enemy or anything else poison or bait us into belief with lies and deceits.

I can live in a perpetual springtime, a place of life and fruitfulness as I live in tender sensitivity to the revelation of who He is and what He says about me. Then I am not living "under" the circumstances of my season; rather, I am living in strength, quiet confidence, faith and from a place of victory in the revelation of my already-purchased wholeness in Him. I am living in a place of life in every season in my intimacy with Him.

I love what Pastor Bill Johnson says, "I cannot afford to have a thought in my head about myself that He doesn't have about me."

> *We are destroying sophisticated arguments and every exalted and proud thing that sets itself up against the [true] knowledge of God, and we are taking every thought and purpose captive to the obedience of Christ* (2 Corinthians 10:5 AMP).

> *We can demolish every deceptive fantasy that opposes God and break through every arrogant attitude that is raised up in defiance of the true knowledge of God. We capture, like prisoners of war, every thought and insist that it bow in obedience to the Anointed One* (2 Corinthians 10:5 TPT).

We have to be ferocious when guarding our minds and our thought life.

Isaiah 26:3 (NKJV) says: "*You will keep him in perfect peace, whose mind is stayed on You, because he trusts in You.*"

I remember doing a podcast episode with my beautiful friend Courtney Kueck in 2024, and we were talking about this verse. Courtney shared something with me that she had heard the Lord say that really encapsulated this depth of invitation to guard our minds and thought life with ferocity. She heard the Lord say, "*Pay attention to what you're paying attention to.*"

As women of God who are living fully alive, we have to be women who are ferocious in paying attention to what we are paying attention to. How easy is it to let a thought carry you away; and when that thought is not a thought of life and truth, my goodness, you end up in the land of despair, hopelessness, fear, anxiety, etc. To live fully alive is to be a woman who lives with a victorious mind. What do I mean by that? She is one who is ever paying attention to what she is paying attention to and taking every thought captive.

I love what it says in the footnotes of my Spirit-filled Life Bible (NKJV, Third edition, Jack Hayford) about this verse: "Perfect peace is expressed in Hebrew by *shalom, shalom,* a Hebrew method of putting great emphasis on a word. You will keep him in everything the word *shalom* implies; health, happiness, well-being, peace. The word translated *mind* is not the usual Hebrew word, but a word meaning 'creative imagination.' Isaiah's thought is that those whose creative imaginations, the seat of plans and ideas, are firmly founded on the eternal Lord will enjoy *shalom* in all its implications."

Wow! Think about that for a second. Your creative imagination, the seat of plans and ideas, if firmly founded on the eternal Lord, will enjoy *shalom* in ALL its implications.

As women of God living fully alive, we must be women who see our creative imaginations rooted deeply in Jesus and His Word. We must be ones who do not allow thoughts to just "come and go." When negative thoughts come and the thoughts that raise themselves up against the knowledge of the Lord, we must *think again.*

God is drawing us as His daughters into a deeper realm of governing over our minds, and in this new era we are going to see a mighty increase of divine strategy given to those who will seek out the mind of the Lord and His counsel. We strive not to have a victorious mind, we have a victorious mind because we have the mind of Christ (1

Corinthians 2:16) and we renew our minds daily growing further up into the mind of Christ in its outworking in our lives through our focus, our pursuit, and our minds stayed upon Him.

Now let's go a little deeper.

I love in Song of Songs 2:15 (TPT) where it says:

> *You must catch the troubling foxes, those sly little foxes that hinder our relationship. For they raid our budding vineyard of love to run what I have planted within you. Will you catch them and remove them for me? We will do it together.*

That is the very essence of an invitation that requires a response. We have a responsibility to deal with the compromises, the lies that are hidden in our hearts. It is our responsibility to guard our hearts and minds because these nasty pests of lies and compromises will hinder the fruit He wants to bring forth within us from flourishing and growing; they will hinder the fruit of the Spirit from bursting forth from within us.

I love here that it says, "*Will you catch them and remove them for me?*" But it doesn't stop there, He then says, "*We will do it together.*" It's a partnership, a pruning, gardening of the heart process with the Lord.

I love what Brian Simmons writes in *The Sacred Journey* on page 94 about this Scripture passage in Song of Songs 2:

> He is not addressing the "lions" of rebellion but the subtle areas that seem so minor yet capable of wounding our love for Him. There are no little sins to God. There is no area that is off limits to the Holy Spirit. Everything is significant when the Lord speaks to us about it. He will help us and show us where the foxes of compromise hide (Psalm 139:23). Jesus comes to us and says, "It is time for a fox hunt; it is time

to remove those areas of darkness in your heart so that the garden within you is not ruined. We all have little areas that destroy a life of fruitfulness. They are our "blind spots." Each pocket of compromise must be dealt with. Every entanglement and weight upon our souls must be shaken off so that we can run our race with endurance and swiftness.

It is crucial that we allow the Holy Spirit's gaze and dealings in our lives to highlight and expose these foxes in our lives, the revelation of where they are hiding and what they are. We choose no longer to align with those foxes through repentance and changing our mind as we are baptized afresh in the fire of His love and truth and turn away from that "self-life" and walk consecrated to Him and watch His budding fruits of new life flourish within us. We recognize nothing can be done in our own strength; we have responsibility to guard our vineyards of intimacy, the gardens of our hearts and be intentional, but we recognize we do not do it alone, it is by *His Spirit* that we are growing up into wholeness and catching these troubling foxes.

I remember in a very dark season of my life when I was faced with a torment of the mind and demonic attack on a level I had not experienced before. Having a conversation with my good friend Anita Alexander, I remember saying to her that I felt like I wasn't going to make it through the season. It was truly a season when I felt the enemy was trying to take me out in such intensity; and at the same time, the Lord was bringing up lies I had believed about myself and exposing "landing places" for the enemy in my life through those lies that I believed.

I remember her saying a phrase that became a weapon for me in that season and continues to be to this day. She said to me, "Lana, rehearse the rhema." That was a key for me in that season; every time the enemy would come to torment me and try to remind me of his lies, while feeling the areas of my heart being caged under the influence of those lies, I would rehearse His rhema over and over again through meditation and declaration until I saw those things break.

## Divine Defiance

The Lord spoke two words to me recently: "*Divine defiance.*"

I see the Lord raising up a company of women in this hour who are living in a place of divine defiance. They have been branded with fire in the secret place with the Lord, the fire of His burning adoration and love for them, the fire of His Word and His presence that is birthing within them a roar that declares, "I will *not* agree with or settle for *anything less* than what is mine in Christ and what *He* speaks about me and over me."

I see this company of women arising with such fiery conviction in their hearts and in their spirits as they have been conquered by love again and again and again and awakened deeper and deeper to the price that was paid for their wholeness. They are arising now with that ferocious resolve and divine defiance that will *not* settle, align, or agree with anything the enemy is speaking over them or their families. They arise with ferocious faith that defies all the enemy speaks and attempts to throw at them, as they arise in *awakened authority. Awake* to their authority in Christ like never before and arising as dangerous to the enemy's plans, branded as an unstoppable force as they live in deep intimacy with Him and surrender to Him and His ways. They crave and long for His words *every day.*

**Stepping into the invitation into revelation brings wholeness and makes room for His truth.**

> *If you wait at wisdom's doorway, longing to hear a word for every day, joy will break forth within you as you listen for what I'll say. For the fountain of life pours into you every time that you find me, and this is the secret of growing in delight and the favor of the Lord* (Proverbs 8:34-35 TPT).

The whole women God is raising up in this hour are ones who make room for Him to speak. They make room for His truth. They are *women of wisdom.*

They are women who intentionally wait, longing to hear a word for every day. They are searching out the fresh manna that the Lord has for them, daily. They are hungry for His Word and His truth, His revelatory secrets and strategies—and they are ones who love to linger.

## Where Are Those Who Will Linger?

I remember a dream I had a few years ago and all night long the Lord spoke over and over, "*Where are those who will linger? Where are those who will linger? For to those who linger I will entrust the secrets of My heart.*"

That dream branded me and marked me for life. Yes, it speaks of that slow pace and not rushing from His presence and making room to linger in His presence daily, but it also spoke to me of the position of the heart, one who lives perpetually in a "heart lingering" state. Always looking for Him, always seeking to hear His voice, wanting to live deeper and deeper in a sensitivity to what He is doing and saying in each moment. And one who does not rush revelation—one who loves to marinate and meditate upon the words that He is speaking and go deeper into the revelation of what He is speaking that leads to an encounter with His nature, over and over again.

On the journey of growing up into wholeness and making room for His truth in the silence, in the slow, in the stillness, in the lingering is imperative.

As one who learned to "push things down and keep moving on" until the Lord stopped me in my keep-moving-on tracks many years ago to reveal to me how unhealthy that process is, let me tell you, that doesn't work. Eventually things start spilling out the sides and overflowing out of your heart, screaming and crying out for healing and restoration. The Lord taught me over many years the importance of keeping "short accounts" with Him. When you recognize a lie in your heart that you are believing or a thought pattern or attitude, go to the Lord and make room for Him to speak. Allow Jesus to walk into that room where the lie has set up camp and ask for His rhema and His truth.

I love how The Passion Translation says in Proverbs 8:34-35, *"joy will break forth within you as you listen for what I'll say."* The Amplified Bible says, *"Blessed [happy, prosperous, to be admired] is the man who listens to me."*

Can I say it again?

*There is an invitation into revelation that brings wholeness.*

There is joy, there is blessing found in finding wisdom. Listening to what He has to say and embracing that rhema with all that we have, not rushing passed it, but making room for His truth, daily.

One word out of His mouth...changes everything!

God is raising up a company of women with *powerful voices* in this hour to release His heart, His truth, His love, His kindness, and His gospel with fire and great authority, because they have found His voice in some of the hardest and darkest of places, some of the most intense seasons, and they have testimonies of how His voice can change everything. They are now arising and being used to declare and decree His truths and His rhema to bring shift and change and see the Kingdom of God and His governmental rule established.

> **Stepping into the invitation into revelation brings wholeness and invites His searching, not yours.**
>
> *Search me [thoroughly], O God and know my heart; test me and know my anxious thoughts; and see if there is any wicked or hurtful way in me, and lead me in the everlasting way* (Psalm 139:23-24 AMP).
>
> *God, I invite your searching gaze into my heart. Examine me through and through; find out everything that may be hidden within me. Put me to the test and sift through all my anxious cares. See if there is any path of pain I am walking on, and lead me back to your glorious, everlasting way—the path that brings me back to you* (Psalm 139:23-24 TPT).

Stepping into the invitation in revelation that brings wholeness, invites His searching, not yours. On the journey of "growing up into wholeness," it is *so* easy to go looking for things. "Where does this come from?" "What is the root of this?" And that "naval gazing" position never leads to hope, it never leads to life, it never leads to faith.

We can look at the fruit in our lives, and when we see bad fruit, if we deal with the fruit and not the root, the bad fruit will come again. God is the God who goes after the root. He is the One who wants to draw us into a place of growing up into complete wholeness and freedom that is already ours in Christ, and to do that, the roots must be dealt with.

## The Fruit of Fear

I remember an encounter I had many years ago that came after seeing the fruit of fear in my life in a big way. It was a root of fear that was affecting many areas of my life and was a space of deep torment for me. I went to the Lord and I invited *His* searching gaze. I asked the Holy Spirit to find where that pathway of pain I was walking on began, I asked Him to set me free.

The Lord immediately took me back into a memory from my childhood. Now let me be honest, I was *very* hesitant when I saw that in this vision we were about to enter into the room where there had been a lot of pain for me. But I remember in that moment feeling the protection of Jesus standing with me. He wasn't leading me back into this place to see me traumatized again, or to cause me pain again, He was bringing me back into this place because it had become a landing place of the enemy and a place of deep pain in my life. So in we went.

We took the first step in and although I could feel some of the pain and fear in that memory, the Lord was shielding me from the intensity of what I had experienced in that room as a young girl. As we walked into the center of the room, Jesus grabbed my hands and He looked into my eyes and spoke His words of truth. I remember in the natural, sobbing and sobbing as His words of love and truth washed over me and deliverance and healing and freedom were taking place.

I was being conquered by love *again*. His words washed over me and that room, where black had covered the walls, started to turn back to gold. He was redeeming. He was healing. He was reminding me again of my original design in my identity in Christ, and I grew up a little more into wholeness in that moment. His voice, changed everything. His love, changed everything. A place of deep pain and shame, now a place of life and healing.

As the vision was ending, Jesus held my hand and walked me out of the room that was no longer filled with pain and shame, but now full of life and redemption, and He closed the door. He turned and on the door He drew a big circle and in the middle He wrote, "*Jesus was here.*" When I looked at the door, He had written it in His blood, because it is by His wounds and by His stripes I am healed and I am whole.

That memory, that room of my heart now is no longer one I shy away from, it is one that is now marked as a place of one of my most beautiful encounters with Jesus, because my life was changed by seeing again what happens when He speaks and what happens when He walks in the room—everything changes.

He brought up that memory, He brought up that pain not to leave me there and have me sit in it—He brought it up to bring it out. To set me free and grow me up more and more into wholeness. It was "unto something" and it is always "unto something." It is "unto healing," it is "unto life," it is "unto wholeness," it is "unto fruitfulness," it's "unto living *fully alive.*"

Daughter of God, whole woman, if we are to be women who are living fully alive in Christ, we are to be ones who are walking in wholeness as we daily accept the invitation into the revelation of who He is and what He is speaking that brings wholeness.

It is time for the labels to come off you. It's time for the containments to be broken off you. It's time for you to flourish in wholeness like never before. It's time for you to walk in freedom and power like never before as you step into the invitations into revelation that bring wholeness.

Arise, woman, daughter of God living *whole and fully alive*. Your day of destiny has arrived.

# 4

# LIVING THE ASCENDED LIFE

Being a wife to an amazing man, a mama to four incredible children ranging from 15 years old down to 1 year old, homeschooling three of them, running an international ministry, podcasting, and hosting online schools, life is very full, gloriously full. But the hours and hours I used to have when I had only one child to sit in my prayer room and listen to what the Lord was saying, I don't have in this season. Though I long for those long hours again, sitting with the Lord and listening to His heart, I am now in a different season, a wonderfully beautiful full season, a different season; but He, my beautiful Jesus, still remains the same. Never changing!

I often am asked the question, "Lana, how do you have time with Jesus with such a full family and life?" And for many years it would really get me down that I just didn't have the capacity or the time like I used to have, a revelation of something the Lord spoke to me in my first few years walking with Him was concreted deeper than ever in the current season I find myself: *"Lana, I want to speak to you, more than you want to listen."* I remember hearing Him speak those words to me and they brought me such comfort. He was revealing Himself to me as the Pursuer. He was revealing His heart to me that He longs for communion and conversation with me, more than I do and more than I want to listen.

The Lord began to awaken in my heart the revelation of how present He is with me, all the time, and how He wants to speak to me *throughout* my day, not just the time I would have before Him, sitting in silence in my prayer room.

So I began to look for Him everywhere. I remember realizing then that being with Him and lingering in His presence wasn't just the physical space of sitting in my beautiful prayer room that I had set up to meet with Him, it was a heart posture, it was a posture that looked for Him and longed to commune with Him *throughout* my day. It broke me out of a "religious" box that said it had to look a certain way. He invites me into the depths of discovering Him as I go about my day, every day.

So over the years, the hunger and awakening began to flourish in me more and more to look for Him everywhere. To commune with Him and listen to what He is speaking *throughout* my day.

The invitation that was extended to me in the revelation that He wants to speak to me more than I want to listen, leading me into a place of knowing and discovering Him in every part of my day that I walked deeper and deeper into, I find myself now as a mama to four beautiful kiddos and a full and beautiful life, so thankful for.

Why do I tell you all of that? Because what I am about to tell you happened at my kitchen sink. That's right, you read that right, my kitchen sink. I met Him. As I washed the dishes to serve my family, I met Jesus. He walked right on into my kitchen. His presence so tangible, so weighty, that I had to hold on to the sink to keep myself standing.

He interrupted my evening. He reminded me again that He is the Lover of my soul and the relentless Pursuer of my heart. This night, I was surrounded again with the depth of revelation of His desire to speak to me.

I felt Him lean in close and He spoke the words, "*Many of My daughters have become accustomed to living in constant battle mode, now they shall become accustomed to living ascended.*"

In that moment, the Lord began to show me the areas of my life where I had become "accustomed" to living in constant battle mode. I had been through so many battles over the years, in what was back-to-back battle, that my heart had come to expect the battles. In that moment I realized that I had been living my life waiting for the next battle, anticipating the next round of warfare or the next thing I would have to push through, and the Lord showed me that somehow in the midst of what I had experienced in the natural, I began to form this expectation and this belief in my heart (that was not the heart of the Lord) that it would never change and that I would always be living in "fight or flight" mode.

## Further Into Freedom

I didn't even realize there were parts of my heart that were occupying that space. The Lord is so wonderful in all of His ways; and the way He speaks to bring forth things that are containing and caging us, to bring us further into freedom, is simply stunning. In that moment the Lord was not revealing that I had become accustomed to living in battle mode to condemn me, He spoke it to bring me further into freedom as an invitation into ascension, living in and from the higher place in Him.

A short while after that encounter I had a dream, and in my dream I was waiting in a room to be enlisted onto the battlefield. I was waiting for my name to be called to go out again, when someone stood before me. I couldn't see anyone in front of me but I knew someone was there. The person placed both of their hands on my shoulders and turned me in the opposite direction, so now my back was to the door I thought I was about to walk through to be enlisted again, when I saw another door in front of me.

I was gently led into this new room, and it was the most beautiful bridal chamber. The words then surrounded me, "*off the battlefield into the bridal chamber.*" There was such a deep sense of rest in the bridal chamber. Such a sense of peace and deep intimacy. I then heard the words, "*Where the battle has wearied you, I am bringing you back to wonder in the bridal chamber,*" and I woke up.

I realized after that dream just how much the weariness of battle had shifted my perspective and how I was viewing things and my posture of expectation in some ways. He was bringing me back to the place of wonder of who He is and the deep place of rest and peace found in the place of intimacy. The Lord was highlighting my perspective and my expectation and bringing me back into alignment to come up higher than ever before.

Back to the encounter in my kitchen.

That one sentence the Lord spoke was an invitation into revelation and into His heart. So I responded. I stopped and I listened.

I leaned into Him to hear His heart, and I heard Him speak:

> *Lana, there are many of My daughters, yourself included, who have become accustomed to living in constant battle mode. The trials and hardships, the warfare and the onslaughts that you have been facing have left many of you feeling like you are living in high levels of fight or flight. Many of you are feeling more battle weary than ever. Many of you are carrying a burden of exhaustion, but I say unto you, I am* ***roaring over you!*** *I am roaring over you and the* ***roar of My authority*** *is awakening you to* ***My authority*** *within you. As I am roaring over you there is a great alignment taking place. There is a great awakening taking place in your life and My* ***roar*** *is releasing strength and life to every part of your being. This is not something for you to strive for, this is a supernatural move of My Spirit that is bringing divine strength, empowerment, and resurrection power into your lives.*

He continued to speak:

> *As I roar I am* ***rewiring*** *your perspective. For many of you have become so accustomed to battle that your expectations have become aligned with warfare. Your expectations have become aligned with hardship. Your expectations have become aligned with "I will always be living in this level of battle. From battle to battle." But I say unto you My daughters,* ***No!*** *You will live from* ***glory to glory*** *and* ***strength to strength.***
>
> *For there is a mighty deliverance taking place over your lives right now. There is a mighty shift taking place in your life where I am moving you* ***out of weariness*** *and* ***back into wonder.***

There it is! My dream! Out of weariness and back into wonder. The Lord is lifting off the heavy burdens, He is lifting off the deep weariness and exhaustion that many daughters of God have lived in and felt like they were drowning in, and He is *restoring wonder.* He is realigning and rewiring and bringing His daughters back into the place of wonder, the wonder of who He is and that our intimacy with Him, as Graham Cooke says, our greatest weapon against the enemy is that we *know* who He is, His nature, His power, His love, His faithfulness. We know *who* we are and *whose* we are.

## Ascended Living

The Lord continued to speak:

> *Many have felt as if you have been living "under" everything for so long. You have felt like you are living as the tail and not as the head; but I say unto you,* ***you are the head, not the***

*tail. I am bringing you into a place of greater authority that you already have in Me,* ***by faith****, as I reveal to you* ***afresh*** *where you are seated. For now is the time for you to become* ***accustomed to living ascended****. For I am bringing you up and out of what has held you down. I am bringing you* ***up and out*** *of what has tried to steal your joy, steal your voice, and steal your strength. I am* ***infusing you*** *in your innermost being and even down to your cellular level with My supernatural strength.*

*For where many of you have felt like you are constantly feeling like you are "living under" and "waiting for the next battle," always "on alert" and on guard, I say unto you,* ***enter My rest****. For I am speaking to your very soul, I am speaking to your very heart* ***"Peace, be still!"*** *I am bringing you deeper into a place of divine rest in* ***who I am****. The revelation of who I am as* ***King*** *is flooding your life, afresh. Get ready to be baptized afresh in the revelation of who I am as* ***Victor and King****. I am baptizing you afresh in the fire of My presence that will awaken you in greater ways to who I am as Victor and King.* ***I have already overcome!***

*I am roaring over you:* ***"Be released! Be released! Be released! Be re-introduced to My power!"***

This mighty deliverance of the Lord and divine aligning of perspective is bringing His daughters further into what it means as a woman of God to live, fully alive. A woman of God who lives fully alive is a woman who lives the ascended life. She is the one who is growing up into *knowing* where she sits (Ephesians 2:6), *knows* her place of authority, *knows* the place of rested faith, and most importantly knows who *He* is and who He is for—*her.*

The Lord's heart is for you to live *accustomed* to living the ascended life. There is a place of victory that the Lord is bringing His daughters into, it's the place of victory from the place of intimacy. It's a place of victory knowing we are *already* victorious in Christ because of what *He* has conquered, what *He* has purchased, and what *He* has done. A mighty shift is taking place, daughter of God, where the Lord is shifting you further into living from a place of victory, rather than living under or feeling like you are living on the defense rather than on the offense.

The Lord is calling us to ascend His mountain. To become accustomed with living the ascended life. We ascend the mountain of the Lord with clean hands and a pure heart (Psalm 24). What we put our hands to and the intentions of our heart are all toward Him in purity, in worship, in first-love fire. Throwing off anything that we have elevated above Him, any idols, any adoration before Him, things that have overtaken the affection of our hearts greater than Him. We offer our lives again on the altar with a cry that all we do is from the place of giving all glory, honor and praise unto Him. That He is our Beloved, He is our First Love, He is our all in all, and from that place we ascend, worshipping in spirit and in truth.

I see an army of women ascending the mountain of the Lord. They are ascending blazing with first-love fire in this hour. They are no longer contained, they are no longer hindered, they are walking and ascending *from* wholeness and *into* wholeness. They are ascending *from* the place of worship *into* greater realms of worship of their beautiful Jesus. They are singing in one accord, in oneness together as an army, a sisterhood of burning ones, who are arising with a song bursting forth from their heart, and it is a song of praise as they burn more and more for their Beloved. The One whose eyes are like flames of fire. They are ascending the mountain of the Lord no longer bent over, heads down and weary—with each step they take they are being infused with spiritual strength, divine order is manifesting in their lives, and the justice of the Lord is bringing recompense to them for what they have endured.

These daughters of God are being strengthened again. They are blazing, blazing with a song of high praise as they awaken further and further into the revelation of their *oneness* in Christ. As they march together, not competing, not fighting against one another, but in *one accord* as they live deeper and deeper in their oneness with Jesus. Chains are falling off. Lies that have held them captive for so long are suddenly being exposed. Weary knees and hands are strengthened and swords picked up again with a roar and fire in their eyes that declares, "*I know my avenging King and I know who I am*"—and the roar comes from a deep place of dependence. It comes from such a deep place of yielding to Him, they arise in strength. Strength not of this world—*His strength*.

This mighty army, this company of women, growing up further and further into the revelation of their destiny and purpose to *know Him* and make Him known, living fully alive in Him, is taking over *every area* where the enemy tried to kill them. Brokenness tried to take them out, weariness almost stopped them, foxes in their vineyards or double-mindedness entrapped them—but they are now *ascending!* Insecurity is losing its hold. Comparison is being shaken off. Authority is flourishing from the deep places of humility, surrender and knowing His ways, being moldable and pliable in His hands, they are arising in authority. Not for their own fame or name, but for the *glory of His!* Here they come, they arise to shine (Isaiah 60), they arise to take their place on earth, and they arise to govern with Him like never before.

## Look Up, Look Forward

Daughter of God, listen to me. In Him, nothing is lost. Nothing is wasted. It's time to *look up and look forward.* Do *not* look back.

The Lord is speaking, *"Eyes up! Eyes front."* This is your call to action with no distraction. There has been much attempting to tug at you in many directions and vying for your attention and focus. Do not look behind you. Do not turn around and look back at your past and long for what was. As you ascend the mountain of the Lord in this hour with a mighty army, a company of laid-down, Jesus-loving daughters of God around you, *look up!*

We are in a very significant time in the body of Christ right now, and there is a very specific direction and divine intel that the Lord is releasing. The Lord is calling you to ascend and come up higher, and part of that coming up higher is coming out of the old season, out of the ashes and into beauty (Isaiah 61). Coming up out of living by what is seen in the natural realm and coming up higher in seeing as He sees in an unprecedented way. There is a laying aside of all things that have hindered, and ascending the mountain of the Lord is this first-love adoration.

As we ascend the mountain of the Lord together, I hear the Lord say, *"Steward your sight."* Now more than ever, it is imperative that as God's people we are aligning ourselves with how He sees.

Colossians 3:2 (AMP) says: *"Set your mind and keep focused habitually on things above [the heavenly things], not on the things that are on the earth [which have temporal value]."*

I hear the Lord say:

> *As you ascend, as you come up higher, do not grieve what was. Do not look back with longing of what was. Do not allow distraction in your midst because of what is happening or has happened around you. It is time to look up. Look up higher. Part of living as a woman of God fully alive, is living as one who lives with her eyes up. Look forward with great expectation, for I am inviting you into partnering with Me*

*in great exploits. Look to Me. Lift up your eyes and behold Me and cultivate great expectation within your heart for what is to come in Me and what I am doing in your midst, for My glory is upon you. My power and glory will be revealed in greater ways than you have ever seen. Draw close to Me and listen to the words of My heart speaking over you. It's time to let go of what was and embrace the expansion. Part of the ascension is letting go of what was and embracing what I am releasing. Embracing what I am doing.*

***Eyes up! Eyes front!*** *The only time you are to look back is to* ***rejoice in what I have done*** *and to remember My great works. As you steward your sight and your expectation in faith, holiness, hope, and purity, oh what a fragrant offering it is to Me.* ***I am not standing on the sideline,*** *I am present with you. Ask Me to help you steward your sight, for it is not by might, nor by power but by My Spirit. You* ***must be vigilant*** *in your vision.* ***Vigilant in your vision!***

***Eyes up! Eyes front!*** *This is my call to action! I am aligning My army! I am gathering My army and slinging you in ferocious focus to move into all I have for you and to partner with Me to see My glory and My name manifest on earth. I am raising up a* ***focused*** *Bride who beholds Me and lives in the ferocious focus of faith and sees as I see.* ***Eyes up! Eyes front,*** *for you are entering unprecedented days of seeing Me, revelation of My Word, divine intel and strategies to build with Me, govern with Me and see My glory come.*

The word *govern* surrounded me so strongly as the Lord spoke. As I leaned in and listened, I heard the Lord say:

*My daughters, you shall govern with Me in this hour like never before. I am going to teach you and train you to govern with Me in ways you have never experienced and in ways you have never walked in. I am calling you up higher. Oh how you shall walk with Me into deeper revelation of My Word and higher places of My revelation to govern with Me in the nations of the earth. There are sacred strategies flowing from My heart that will flow unto you as you sit at My feet.*

*Many of you have faced such an intense battle over your vision. Confusion has tried to steal from your vision, but I say unto you now in the ascending by the empowerment of My Spirit and your posture of purity intimacy with Me, you shall* ***see*** *clearer than you have ever seen. You shall be trained by My Spirit in a greater way how to live, operate, and move in* ***My*** *authority, divine intel, and strategy, from the place of deep intimacy and surrender to* ***see My glory come!***

*You shall see strategic intel given to you for intercession. You shall govern with Me through your prayers and intercession. Through your declaration and decree of what you see* ***in*** *Me and* ***through*** *Me. I am positioning you as My divine midwives in this hour to come alongside others and help them birth My plans, purposes, and promises. I am bringing you deeper into* ***My heart*** *to partner with Me to birth through intercession* ***My ways*** *on earth. For I will give you* ***My keys*** *to see things suddenly turn around, to see My divine power suddenly intervene, and to see My glory come. There are many keys waiting for you especially in the areas you have been contending in. For I declare over you* ***suddenly.*** *In this hour, in areas where there has been great contending and it has felt long and hard, I say unto you as you receive My keys* *of divine intel and intercede, you shall see things* ***suddenly come into being!***

*I am calling you deeper into prayer and intercession in this hour, and I am calling you up higher, to ascend,* ***see and speak from your seat.*** *As you live closer to My heart and yielded to Me, you shall receive wisdom; continue to ask for wisdom and discernment and it shall be given to you. I shall give divine strategy to My friends like never before. You will know what it means to live the victorious ascended life* **in Me,** *as you draw close to Me (James 4:8).*

*It's time to ascend (Psalm 24), it's time to come up higher. Know that you will no longer be held down by what has tried to kill you, squash you, contain you and suffocate you, it's time to fly!*

*Healing oil is flowing. A wave of My healing is flowing. Many of you—My daughters who have faced an onslaught of attack against your physical bodies, your minds, and your hearts—watch how My healing power is flowing to you to bring greater healing and wholeness and watch the birthing and releasing of My healing oil* ***through you*** *to see Me reveal Myself as Jehovah Rapha to those around you and* ***into your home.***

*For many of you have faced onslaught in your home and many mothers have experienced constant sickness in their homes with their children and I say unto you,* ***arise*** *and declare My healing over your home again, for not only am I bringing a breaking to the onslaught of the enemy in your home, I am going to release My healing oil through* ***you, your children,***

> ***your family, your household to see*** *My healing oil fill the streets, into your neighborhoods and other homes* ***through you.***

Daughter of God, it's time to live fully alive in greater and greater ways. It is time to arise and ascend and become accustomed to living the ascended life in Christ. It's time for you to take your place in a greater way. Sure there will be battles in life, but you will not be living in the expectation of living battle weary. The Lord is awakening His daughters to what it looks like to live the ascended life in Christ. Supernatural peace, joy, strength, faith, and found in Him that lives *from* a place of victory. It doesn't mean we don't get tired at times, and the battle rages fiercely, but we battle from the place of victory and from a place of *rest* knowing who He is, who goes before us, goes with us, and who we are living *in* and *from* Him all strength, peace, and life flows.

The world needs women of God living dangerously awake in Him and living fully alive in Him from a place of supernatural peace and strength. He is working deeply within you in this hour, causing you to arise and understand in greater ways what it means to live the ascended life in Christ.

5

# A WOMAN OF GOD LIVING FULLY ALIVE IS HERE TO HEAR

In this hour on a global scale, we are seeing God raise up an army of daughters who are rising up in such boldness in Him; their days of cowering are over, and they are stepping into the days of seeing God move through them in divine power in unprecedented ways.

I heard the Lord say: "*I am looking for humility. To live fully alive is to live in deep humility.*"

I love Matthew 16:24-25 (NKJV):

> *Then Jesus said to His disciples, "If anyone desires to come after Me, let him deny himself, and take up his cross and follow Me. For whoever desires to save his life will lose it, but whoever loses his life for My sake will find it."*

These two Scripture verses speak deeply to me of humility. The denying of oneself in humility to take up our cross and follow Him, not desiring to save our life but in the losing of our life, the laying down in humility of all that we are and all of our life, we find our life in Him.

To live fully alive is to deny ourselves, take up our cross, follow Him, and lose our self-centered life. To live fully alive, is to live in humility.

I remember the many encounters I have had leading up to the entry of this new era where I saw the eyes of the Lord roaming the earth looking for those whose hearts were fully devoted to Him (2 Chronicles 16:9) and living before Him in humility and purity. They were not ones seeking fame or their own name, but consumed with fiery unadulterated love for Him as their First Love, their greatest desire was that His name would be glorified on earth.

I remember in one of those encounters specifically for the daughters of God, hearing the Lord say: "*These ones are not here for their names to be seen, they are not here to parade revelation, they are* ***here to hear.***"

Oh daughter of God, those words, ***"They are here to hear,"*** when He spoke those words I heard the thundering of His voice and I saw the *thundering* of the feet of the army of His daughters arising.

The women God is raising up in this hour, living fully alive, they live *fully alive* because they live to *hear* His voice. They live deeply in a place of Matthew 4:4 (AMP):

> *But Jesus replied, "It is written and forever remains written, 'Man shall not live by bread alone, but by every word that comes out of the mouth of God.'"*

I love this verse deeply. It is one of my life verses and a verse that truly encapsulates one of the strongest passions of my heart—to live by every word that flows out of the mouth of God.

Then I heard it again, the sound of the thundering of feet, the thundering of the army, and they were all saying in one accord: "It is written and forever remains written. His Word endures forever. His Word endures forever."

When Jesus speaks in Matthew 4:4, He is referencing Deuteronomy 8:3 (NKJV):

> *So He humbled you, allowed you to hunger, and fed you with manna which you did not know nor did your fathers know, that He might make you know that man shall not live by bread alone; but man lives by every word that proceeds from the mouth of the Lord.*

So He is saying it is written and will always be that you live not just by bread alone, but you live every day feasting, eating, receiving the manna, the word that comes out of the mouth of God, for you, daily.

As the army of daughters marched forth, I heard the authority and conviction within them, *nothing* can change His Word. His Word *remains!* His Word is true! His Word *endures.* The daughters of God were marching upon the never-changing, living, breathing, *alive* Word of God and rhema words that flow from His mouth and revelation of His nature within His Word, that *can never* be shaken, *ever.*

These daughters of God whom the Lord is causing to arise in this hour are living fully alive, because they hunger, they deeply hunger, are ravenously hungry for His Word and to hear His voice, they are *here to hear* and then release His voice on earth.

He spoke again:

> *Their greatest desire is to know Me and hear My voice. Watch these ones arise from the wilderness in this hour and they arise with swords in their mouths. They arise with the sword of My Spirit in their mouths to speak and decree that which is of Me and to see My Word separate between what is not of Me and what is of Me. They come with My Word in their mouths, carrying My heart and declaring My Word that brings the intensity of My voice, the thunderings of My heart that brings*

> ***catalytic change.*** *They will not apologize for what I speak, they will speak in obedience, declaring My Word with power and authority.*

You may be called to be a prophet or you may not be, but the truth is we have all been given a voice that the Lord wants to use. He wants His Words and His truth to flow from your mouth; and in this hour, the Lord is calling you to raise your voice and speak. To speak as He prompts you to speak. To speak words of life, love, encouragement, hope, revelation, insight, and truth. The Lord is moving mightily among His daughters in this hour and causing their voices to arise in boldness in ways we have not seen before. There is a boldness that is and will be required that will come upon you more and more in this hour for you to speak as *He* is leading you. It's time for the daughters of God to arise and speak in greater ways.

The justice of the Lord and the hammer of His Word is going to be seen in this hour through many of His daughters as they arise to protect, defend, and stand for His truth.

## The Mama Bear Roar

The Mama Bear roar is rising on earth to arise, protect, and defend the next generation and generations and stand boldly for truth and for Kingdom values on earth and areas of influence, to bring transformation for the Kingdom of God. There is a groan and heralding of the intercessors, the heralding of the watchmen, the songs of the psalmists and the worshippers, the voice of the Lord through the scribes, the thunderings through the prophets, the bold declarations of truth through the mothers over their children and homes. The faith of the daughters who refuse to move from what His Word says, His voice through the teachers, the gospel through the evangelists, on and on and on it goes—the point being, *your voice matters* and Heaven is calling you to arise and *stand* and use your voice in this hour.

No more timidity, no more shame, no more hiding, no more doubt, no more insecurity, *arise* daughter of God, *arise* warring woman of Zion and take your place afresh. For you are being baptized into boldness in this hour as you live in the secret place before Him, the deliverance of fear of man is taking place and God is preparing you and positioning you to arise with the thunder of His voice and the sword of the Spirit in your mouth. God is moving powerfully to awaken His daughters to the power of their declaration and decree and the influence of His voice through their lives.

Where many have faced years and years of having their voice shut down or being told their voice is wrong, the Lord is severing ties to those lies and those seasons and causing His daughters to arise living fully alive as they hear His voice and His Spirit moving within them to increase the fire of faith. In this hour they will find themselves speaking because they are living so deeply in communion with Him and revelation of who He is.

In Jeremiah 20:9 we see a cry from Jeremiah that if he does not mention the name of the Lord and speak His name anymore, it is like a burning fire shut up in his bones that he cannot contain any longer. Jeremiah, a prophet, was called to speak and prophesy, and in the context of this Scripture, his message from the Lord was met with hostility. Yet even when he wants to stop speaking, he cannot. There is a boldness and a courage seen here that I believe is a prophetic picture of the type of boldness and courage that the Lord is igniting and increasing within His daughters in this hour.

> *If I say, I will not make mention of [the Lord] or speak any more in His name, in my mind and heart it is as if there were a burning fire shut up in my bones. And I am weary of enduring*

> *and holding it in; I cannot [contain it any longer]* (Jeremiah 20:9 AMPC).

I love this Scripture verse because it is a beautiful example of what happens when identity in the Lord and who He has made us to be overtake the insecurity, fear, and rejection. It is a picture of what it looks and feels like when He expands to fill us so fully that His message cannot be contained, it must be spoken.

## A New Level of Intercession

In Chapter 4, "Living the Ascended Life," we looked at how the Lord is positioning His daughters in this hour as midwives to come alongside others and help them birth His plans, purposes, and promises and how He is releasing specific intercession to see His power intervene and His glory come on earth. Ascending further into the realm of governing with Him.

I want us to dive into this space of intercession again, as I hear the Lord speaking: *"I am igniting intercession...**groan!** I am igniting intercession...travail. **Birth, birth, birth in boldness. Birth in boldness."***

The Lord began to speak to me about the boldness that the daughters of God will walk in. In this hour it is the boldness of being unapologetic for the burden of the Lord that they carry and how they carry it.

For the Lord says:

> *There are burdens and birthings being released upon My daughters in this hour and era. There are burdens and birthings. Do not water down the **sound** of My burden and the **sound** of My birthing. For through your intercession, through*

*your groan and through your travail I will birth what you have not seen before and what has not been seen before. I am looking for those daughters in this hour who will allow My Spirit to pray through them in the way that I desire in private or in public. To allow the groan and travail of My heart to come forth and will not hinder or stop* **My cry** *and* **My roar** *for fear of humankind. They will surrender to the groan, they will surrender to the birth and allow My intercession to come forth. They will allow My intercession to flow forth. They will allow* **My** *words to come forth and be* **unashamed,** *for they know they are birthing the* **Kingdom purpose.**

*I am drawing a line in the sand in this hour and asking My daughters, are you all in? Are you all in to carry the burdens of My heart no matter what it looks like? For I am igniting a fire within you that cares more for the weight and privilege of carrying My burden and birthing it on earth that may offend others, in order to see My Kingdom come. The words that I speak in intercession may offend, they may be out of the box, but they remain in the bounds of My Word—the expression of My heart and* **My cry** *may offend many minds. Are you all in? Will you carry My heart no matter what it costs you? This is the call. This is the place. This is the line in the sand.*

*Do you want My heart more than human accolades? It's time to choose! For I am releasing burdens of My heart that are so deep, I am releasing divine intel and secrets of My heart that are so weighty, I entrust them alone to My friends. For the divine intel I am releasing in this hour is not to be paraded but stewarded and carried in direction and leading of My Spirit. Watch the continued increase of groaning intercession that I am birthing within them. These ones arising in this hour as spiritual midwives to birth in intercession the plans, purposes, and divine strategy of My heart for the earth will have an increase of supernatural vision that they have not walked in before.*

*The test of the hour to carry My burden and My birthings is the "need to be seen." For yes, great birthings, groans, and travailing will be carried and be seen and will require boldness, but some great shifts in nations and places will not be seen by all, but only with Me in the secret place. For where there has been some impurity in intercession to gain accolades or to "be seen" when prayer is answered, I am bringing a divide by My fire. I am drawing those who truly seek to carry My heart and partner with Me in intercession, those who are awakened to the privilege to carry My heart and pray with Me to see My glory fall into a greater place of divine intel and intercession.*

*Daughters of My heart, I am inviting you deeply into My heart and into My eyes. What you will hear and what you will see, you have not seen before. What I will reveal in divine strategy is unlike anything you have ever seen. As you seek Me and behold Me in intimacy and humility, I am bringing you into a realm of supernatural mystery and divine understanding with keys in your hand,* **My keys** *that through intercession and the decree of My Word you are being commissioned to go forth with an anointing to* **unleash and unlock** *all I want to release on earth.*

*Daughters of God, I am bringing you deeper into* **My mind!** *For I say unto you that from your kitchens, mothers and wives, you shall see strategy beyond your understanding as* *you step further into My mind to* ***clearly*** *see My strategy for intercession. Daughters of God, divine understanding, discernment, and supernatural mysteries will be unlocked to you in this hour for intercession, for strategy and to be* ***conduits*** *of My divine wisdom. For I shall move in power through you in intercession and wisdom to bring* ***catalytic change.*** *I will position you in places you never thought you would step, to release My wisdom.*

*For some of My daughters will sit before kings and leaders and interpret their dreams and deliver the word of the Lord to shift a nation. Others will shift nations from your home through your intercession. Mothers, you are going to another level of divine wisdom and understanding to shepherd, disciple, and train your children. Daughters of God, wherever I the Lord send you in this hour, there is great increase in divine wisdom, supernatural sight, and divine mysteries that I am releasing to you, as you sit at My feet and seek and listen, to go forth in intercession to see My glory and Kingdom manifest.*

*For there are hammers in your hands, daughters of God. Anointed to bring My justice in this hour. Pay* ***close*** *attention to My voice and to the assignments of intercession I am giving to you, for at times I will have you* ***lift and raise your voice*** *in prophetic unction and declare My Word, bringing forth My Word like a hammer that will bring* ***divine justice*** *into manifestation. When these moments come, do not shy away. Stand tall and know that I am with you and that the boldness you require is upon you,* ***because*** *you have been with Me and live in Me.*

*This is just the beginning of living fully alive in Me, what you are going to see and what I will entrust to you in the place of intercession to carry and birth My heart. The deeper place of co-laboring with Me and carrying My heart will cause you to come alive in Me and in your destiny in a way you have not experienced before.*

Daughter of God, from one daughter of God to another, this is not a new season for you, it's a new era. Do not look back to what was (Isaiah 43:18-19), lift up your head. The Lord is gathering His army and we are arising with thunder in our steps—His thunderings in our lives and through our lives. The thunderings of fear will no longer hinder you.

Can I pose the question to you that the Lord posed to me?

*My daughter, could it be possible that I am raising up a company of women in this hour who are fearless and fear is no longer part of the equation or conversation? As I raise up an army of daughters who know that all they need is Me, and* ***nothing is impossible?***

I wholeheartedly believe it. A fearless army of women arising, a ferociously bold company of women arising on earth, carrying His heart, His burdens, His travails, His groans, and His Word—proclaiming it with His power and His authority and making room for His glory.

They are arising—and you, my fellow sister in Christ, are part of this great army.

Take your place!

For such a time as this!

His Word, through you, will cause armies to be conquered!

> *God Almighty declares the word of the gospel with power, and **the warring women of Zion deliver its message:** "The conquering legions have themselves been conquered. Look at them flee!" Now Zion's women are left to gather the spoils* (Psalm 68:11-12 TPT).

The earth and the Church are waiting for the warring women of Zion to arise, it's happening!

Now is the time.

# 6

# MIGHTY WARRING WOMEN OF THE WORD AND PRAYER

I feel the tenderness and ferocity of the Lord's heart so strongly in this season as He raises up mighty warring women of the Word and prayer. As I have sat with Him, heart to heart, face to face, eye to eye beholding His beauty, and hearing His heart for His beautiful daughters that He is raising up in this hour knowing what it is to live *fully* alive in Him, I heard the Lord say:

> *There is a mighty move of My Spirit in this hour awakening My daughters in greater ways to cause them to arise as women of the Word and prayer in a fiercer, more unapologetic and bold way, than they have ever walked in. Where boldness has been quieted and for some lost, I am raising up a company of women living from their original design, how they were created to live as* **bold** *women of the Word and prayer and finding great strength in Me on and from their knees.*

As the Lord spoke these words, I could feel the magnitude of the move of the Holy Spirit among His daughters in this hour. There was such a strong sense in the Lord's heart of the "unprecedented." This is a word that the Lord has used repetitively to me in the past few years and continues to. So as I meditate and marinate upon the words that the Lord spoke in the previous paragraph, I think of the amazing women of God I have read about in Scripture, and women of God I have read about in history including Kathryn Kuhlman, Aimee Simple McPherson, and others. Women leaders and mothers in the body of Christ who have "trail blazed" and pioneered and have been such bold, unapologetic women of the Lord—and I am inspired. I am deeply thankful for the price they have paid in following Him, the way they *knew* Him. I'm thankfulf for those who are still here with us, who continue to know Him and the way He moved and moves through them.

I remember my grandmother, such a beautiful, strong, fiercely unapologetic, godly, faith-filled woman of God and prayer. How she loved the Word and took the Lord at His Word, and her prayer life was rich. She taught me what it looked like to be a woman who knows and loves Him and takes Him at His Word without apology—if He said it, I believe it, and take that heart posture into the place of prayer. What a mighty woman of God who prayed me into the Kingdom and showed me what fierce resolve in the spirit looks like.

I hold alongside what I've seen, experienced, and read about in the lives of amazing women and what the Lord spoke in the first paragraph of this chapter and the sense of "unprecedented." My heart whispers to Him, "There is more, this is the kairos time to see more than we have ever seen and do more than we have ever done, it's unprecedented. It's never been seen or known before; *that* time has arrived."

The Lord showed me an unapologetic roar that is being birthed in His daughters in this hour by HIS hand and it is the place of resolve that we have talked about in previous chapters. This unapologetic roar is the resolve of not being afraid and living unashamed in taking the Lord at His Word—no matter what that looks like—and praying *bold prayers*.

There are many daughters in this hour who have been feeling like their roar has been hindered because of past experiences, the giants of disappointment and unanswered prayers have been screaming loudly. For many, the taunt of the enemy is in their ears, "See, the Word doesn't work." Daughter of God, if that's you, I hear the Lord thundering to you Isaiah 55:11 (AMP):

> *So will My word be which goes out of My mouth; it will not return to Me void (useless, without result), without accomplishing what I desire, and without succeeding in the matter for which I sent it.*

There is a solidarity of posture upon the Word of God that the Lord is building and birthing in His daughters in this hour, that has been found and is being found in the place of deep wrestle that many have walked through. The tension of feeling like they are living in two different realities—what God has said, and what the natural realm is saying or has said.

## Boldness

I saw many daughters in this hour being "unbound," and when I asked the Lord what they are being unbound from, the Lord spoke to Me saying, "*Disappointment.*" The Lord then began to show me roots of disappointment in the hearts of many daughters in this hour that for some has spanned back decades. I heard the Lord say,

> *I am breaking the* ***decades*** *of disappointment, and I am breaking the* ***derailment*** *disappointment has attempted to cause in the lives of My daughters.*

I began to see that these roots of disappointment in the lives of many daughters of God were infiltrating so many areas of their lives, attempting to derail them from remaining aligned in faith and expectation in the Word of God and who He is.

It was then in my vision that I saw these tentacles of disappointment had bound other areas in the lives of His daughters; and when I looked closer, I saw that disappointment had *bound boldness.* It was then that the Lord's voice came a second time and thundered:

> ***From bound to boldness.*** *Now* ***arise*** *daughters of God and move deeper into Matthew 18:18-20 (AMP): "I assure you and most solemnly say to you, whatever you bind [forbid, declare to be improper and unlawful] on earth shall have [already] been bound in heaven, and whatever you loose [permit, declare lawful] on earth shall have [already] been loosed in heaven. Again I say to you, that if two believers on earth agree [that is, are of one mind, in harmony] about anything that they ask [within the will of God], it will be done for them by My Father in heaven. For where two or three are gathered in My name [meeting together as My followers], I am there among them."*

The sense of the move of the Lord's hand to deal with disappointment and to not only break it, but completely uproot it from the roots from within hearts was *so* deep within my spirit as I watched in this vision. It was a ferocious and tender dealing of the Lord's hand upon disappointment. I could feel the heart of the Lord toward His daughters being bound in disappointment and setting them free and calling them to a higher vantage point.

As He spoke, *"From bound to boldness,"* I knew there was a beautiful, divine exchange happening in this hour of our surrender of disappointments at His feet, to Him breaking the back of disappointment in the lives of His daughters and moving His daughters into greater freedom (Galatians 5:1) and a greater *appointment* of the Lord in this kairos time, to govern with Him from the place of being deeply nestled in the Word, standing upon the Word and praying bold prayers.

Precious sister in Christ, this boldness is not of your own strength. It's not something you can stir up in your works, it's not something you can strive for. The boldness of the Lord coming upon you in this hour comes by the Spirit and from the place of deep intimacy, knowing Him so deeply, knowing who He is, and the fire in your bones that He brings forth.

I hear the Lord saying,

> *You have entered a new day of* ***boldness****, no longer will your expectations and prayers be hindered by disappointment. Jesus is walking into the room and turning the tables on disappointment and inviting you to the table of* ***divine appointment*** *in this hour to partner with Him in realms of prayer and intercession that you've not walked in before.*

This happened in my life a few years ago. It was a season in my life when the Lord began to highlight disappointments in my heart and, boy oh boy, there were more there than I realized. Some stemming back as far as the very early years of my childhood. As the Lord would bring these up, the more I would feel how these heavy sandbags of disappointment in my heart and life had hindered my strength in standing upon His Word and also hindered my prayer life. So one day I took the most painful memory of disappointment to the Lord in prayer. I nervously laid it before Him and I asked Jesus to walk into that disappointment (that took courage because of how painful it was) and to speak His truth.

## Jesus Was Here

I then went into a vision and I saw Jesus walk into the room where this disappointment happened. I could feel His love and His peace so strongly as He entered the room. He began to speak words of such love, comfort, truth, and healing over me. As He did, my heart was becoming less and less tangled and less and less tethered to disappointment. At the end of this encounter, He walked out of the room and my vision then went to the door of this room that He closed. A big red circle was painted on the door and within the circle the words: JESUS WAS HERE. I knew His blood had covered it all and washed away that disappointment, and from that day forward I was free and completely healed of the pain and effects of that deep-rooted disappointment in my life. To this day, I think back on that memory and my heart is filled with the joy of how I met Him there and what happens when He walks into the room of some of our deepest pains and disappointments and sets us free.

He wants to do that for you too. Bring those disappointments to Him, invite Him in. Ask Him to speak and quiet your heart and listen to what He says. He will speak to you in the way that you will hear Him. For me, it was in a vision; to you, it will be in the way that you hear Him. But we must surrender those disappointments and allow Him to minister to our hearts and set us free, not just as a once-off, but an ongoing check in our hearts (Psalm 139:23-24) before Him.

A woman of God living fully alive is a woman who does not allow disappointment to have the final word. A woman of God living fully alive is a woman who when the disappointment comes, chooses to exalt His Word above the disappointment—and a woman of God living fully alive is a woman who hopes in the Lord.

> *...I am the Lord; those who hope in me will not be disappointed* (Isaiah 49:23 NIV).

When I read this verse, I feel the call to hope, not superficial hope but deep hope and trust in who God is. I read this and think of all the times I have been disappointed and I wrestled. Until I wondered one day, what was the source of my disappointment? It didn't happen when or how I expected it to turn out and so I was disappointed. I then felt this call of the Lord to come up higher, that no matter what things looked like, I refuse to move from hoping in who He is and trusting in His way and His will and that His promises *never* fail. They may just not manifest in the way I want or I've expected, but Isaiah 55:11 is the truth.

I had a choice to make and continue to make as I face things in my life. Is the Word of God the ultimate truth or is it not? Does God lie? No, we know that Numbers 23:19 (NLT) says, *"God is not a man, so he does not lie. He is not human, so he does not change his mind. Has he ever spoken and failed to act? Has he ever promised and not carried it through?"*

So I decided to live my life in a way that cultivated hope in my heart and a refusal to lower the truth of the Word of God to meet my experiences or circumstances. I had to embrace the wrestle and not run from it. There I found a place where I was slowly finding myself growing up into hope because of who He is and His faithfulness and because I was being a steward over my own heart and my mind to know that as I *hope* in Him—dying to my own ways and expectations, surrendering to His will, and refusing to move from what He says—I will not be disappointed. Because even when things happen, the enemy attacks, or things don't turn out how I expect, as I look into the eyes of Jesus I see the One who says, *"And we know that God causes everything to work together for the good of those who love God and are called according to his purpose for them"* (Romans 8:28 NLT).

And I know in my life, I allowed disappointment to almost knock me out and take me out completely, because I've viewed situations and circumstances through such earthly eyes that I put a full stop on things and set up camp in disappointment, where, in fact, God had just put a comma, He hadn't finished yet. Or I was so quick to put a full stop on things because I didn't see it from His perspective and it was just taking waaaaay too long in my opinion (haven't we all been there). But then when He does come through and fulfill His Word in His perfect timing, it blows me out of the water in awe of Him.

Then to the times when the enemy has come and stolen, he has killed and destroyed, oh the sting and pain of disappointment—but then to see God's recompense, His restoration and His "causes all things for good" manifest in my life, it has left me in awe again. In all the seasons of my life dealing with disappointments, I have seen Him move time and time again, and I came to that point in my life where I tethered myself to HOPE in HIM no matter what, because *He is good* and His Word *never* fails.

SO, from that place, I pray. That truth changes the way I pray. That deep trust and hope in who He is no matter what, that changes the way I pray. I can pray bold prayers because of what His Word says—and His Word never changes, and who HE is never changes. And the *way* He decides to fulfill His Word? I have to leave that to Him.

## "Not Afraid to Be Holy"

I remember seeing a news report circulating on Instagram of a woman named Charlotte Hall from Ezel, Kentucky, who prayed over her home in 2012. It was said that Charlotte's prayers spared her home while much of a nearby small town, West Liberty, was destroyed by the storm. I remember the authority in Charlotte's voice as she prayed. She told a massive storm cloud to go away in the name of Jesus Christ. She continued to pray, and as she prayed the tornado began to move away from her home, but she had no idea it would move on to West Liberty. Charlotte went on to say that she was praying for the people in West Liberty every night.

A number of things struck me in the interview with Charlotte Hall; she was quoted to say on 9News: "It would lift and come back down and I just kept praying," said Hall, who says she knew better than to stay there, but there was no fear. She refused to leave until the cloud did.

> "I've been through many storms in my life, and I was like, 'Okay God, You're gonna take this.' And I knew He would," she said. (See https://www.9news.com/article/news/weird/woman-prays-the-tornado-away-in-kentucky/73-333814539; accessed January 15, 2025.)

In the video I watched, Hall prayed the tornado away, declaring, "I am not afraid to be holy."

(See https://www.facebook.com/watch/?v=1683717085530712; accessed January 16, 2025.)

She kept praying until the tornado moved away. She refused to leave until the cloud did, and she had *no fear.* She had been through many storms and knows who God is and knew that HE would take the storm and He did.

Then those words, ***"I am not afraid to be holy."***

The unapologetic roar that comes from a heart that knows Him, a friend of God who knows the power of His Word and is not afraid to stand boldly and to be holy in standing in faith no matter how bold it may look; this is the unapologetic roar that the Lord is increasing in His warring women in this hour.

I want to say this, being a warring woman of the Word and prayer is not determined by how loud your roar is. It's not about being loud in the natural, it's about your resolve. It's about your and my resolve to remain grounded and founded in the Word and so deeply intimate with

Him that we know His heart, we know His voice, we know His nature, we know His leading, and we refuse to move. I believe from Charlotte's quote she leaned heavily on her history with God: "I've been through many storms in my life, and I was like, "Okay God, you're going to take this, and I knew He would"—that's history with God.

Disappointment comes and attempts to blind us from our history with God and it steals vision and faith for what God wants to do in the present and the future and ties you up in the lies of "Well, it didn't work out last time, don't pray a bold prayer again, you will be disappointed again." Disappointment tries to give you spiritual amnesia of what God has done in your life in times past and hold you in a place of regret and pain in the areas where disappointment has taken root.

A warring woman of the Word and prayer takes God at His Word with a ferocious faith to stand and not move until we see the Word of God manifest. Remind you of someone in Scripture? Elijah refused to move from the place of intercession in 1 Kings 18 until he saw rain, until the cloud the size of a man's hand arose out of the sea. A warring woman who lives fully alive lives in deep dependence on the Lord and trusts in who He is and what He has said.

God is building *resilience and endurance* in prayer in His daughters like never before as He breaks the back of the stronghold of disappointment in hearts in a deeper way than they have ever experienced.

Where disappointment has kept you bound, the Lord is taking you into such a deeper realm of faith, expectation, resilience, and endurance in prayer that is coming from deeper depths of encounters with Jesus, His heart, and His Word, as you diligently seek Him.

In Psalm 109:4 (TPT) David says, "*Though I love them, they stand accusing me like Satan for what I've never done. I will pray until I become prayer itself.*"

"*In return for my love they are my accusers, but I give myself to prayer*" (Psalm 109:4 NKJV).

In the footnotes of The Passion Translation, Brian Simmons writes: "In the face of accusation and slander, David wrote in Hebrew literally 'I am prayer.'"

These very words here, "I am prayer," absolutely blew me away when I read them. This shows how deeply in the face of accusations and oppression from his enemies, David finds such trust and refuge in the place of prayer and trust in the Lord. As I read the words "I am prayer," what struck me was how these words spoke of being totally overcome and consumed by prayer. It speaks to me of a life so devoted to prayer, that place of praying without ceasing (1 Thessalonians 5:16-18), giving oneself totally over to the place of prayer and its workings *in* you and *through* you, and where prayer has the place of highest priority. It's the recognition of what happens when you pray and the oneness with the Lord the place of prayer evokes.

I want to be, if I can say it this way, "prayer with legs." I want to so deeply carry His heart, His Word, His revelation, and co-labor with Him in the place of prayer that I could carry His secrets and intercessions with the Great Intercessor (Romans 8:34; 1 John 2:1; Hebrews 7:25) to see His purposes, plans, and will extended on earth and live in that oneness of prayer, without apology.

I believe the Lord is raising up His daughters in this hour as houses of prayer, ones who are housing the heart of the Lord in such deep ways and partnering with Him to see His groans and His desires manifested on earth and refuse to move until they see what He has spoken come to pass.

In closing, let's go back to what the Lord says at the beginning of this chapter:

> *I am raising up a company of women living from their original design, how they were created to live as* **bold** *women of the*

*Word and prayer and finding great strength in Me on and from their knees.*

Daughter of God, warring woman, this is a new day for you, to dive into deeper depths. The Lord is awakening you and causing you to *arise* in your *original* design, deeper than you have ever known. You are designed to live *fully* alive in Him, in deep intimacy, hearing His voice, and living as a bold woman of the Word and prayer, finding your strength in Him on your knees in deep dependence, surrender and trust, and from your knees governing with Him in a place of new depths of prayer and intercession in this hour.

May the fire of His Spirit come upon you, baptizing you afresh with boldness.

Arise mighty warring woman of the Word and prayer, this is a new day of you seeing God's power flowing in and through your life and stepping further into living as a woman of God, *fully alive*.

# 7

# "LORD, I WILL WORSHIP YOU WITH MY EXPECTATIONS"

I remember the day when eight words flowed out of my mouth and the weight of His presence fell on me so strongly: *"Lord, I will worship You with My expectations."*

When those words came out of my mouth, I could hardly move. I remember it almost taking my breath away; the anointing on the words was so heavy, it stopped me in my tracks.

That's when I felt the fire of the Lord come upon my heart in such an intense way. I had never even thought of my expectations being a place of worship to Him. But of course, they are; my whole life, every area is worship to Him. I live my life on the altar as a living sacrifice unto Him, and in every area of my life I sing His praises. I knew the fire was being turned up, the Refiner's fire was increasing, and I was being called up higher. There was no condemnation, there was awakening.

I immediately realized those eight words that flowed out of my mouth were an invitation from the Lord to come up higher and to go deeper into His heart. It was an invitation into an abandonment and devotion to Him, even deeper still.

So I began to look at the expectations in my life. Not navel-gazing, but inviting the Holy Spirit to come and examine me in the light of His presence. I invited His searching gaze (Psalm 139:13-14) to come and examine my expectations, and He did just that.

I found as He shone His light on expectations in my heart, that so many of my expectations had become aligned with the effects of previous seasons. There was a grief within me of how my heart had strayed, but there was life in it. Where there had been pain and grief in some areas of my heart, hope deferred had taken up residence. In some parts of my heart where there had been trauma, lies or hiding had set up camp in my heart. I found areas where there was either no hope at all, I had given up, or there were areas where expectations were not founded in the truth of who God is or what His Word says.

## Come Up Higher

I could feel His heart wooing Me, "*Come up and out of these wrong expectations. Come up and out of the places that were empty of expectation and hope. It is time to come up higher.*"

I want you to understand that there was no sense of condemnation, repentance flowed out of me as I was confronted with areas of my heart that had aligned with these effects of previous seasons. The light of the Lord upon my heart was calling me higher and drawing me deeper into freedom.

That "come up higher" was not a place to strive and try to reach. "If I *try* hard enough, then my expectations will increase." No. Rather, it was an invitation to abide. So those very areas where I saw wrong expectations, empty expectations, and where hope deferred had taken up residence, or exhaustion had set up camp, in those areas I had to intentionally abide in Him.

Those areas had to be completely saturated in the beauty of God and the revelation of who He is. I had to make an intentional choice to posture my heart again toward the Son and in faith. *Despite* how I felt.

That's when the voice of the Lord crashed in:

*Many are dancing with their emotions. Many have become emotion led and have postured their hearts for their emotions to lead. Emotions are not wrong, I have given My people emotions, but they are not to lead you. Many are finding their expectations waning because they are giving more voice and airplay to their emotions and how they feel than voice and airplay to My Word. It is time to elevate the unchanging Word, the powerful Word, My Word that is alive and active* **above** *emotions and pick up authority again. While emotions are leading, expectations wane.*

*Where many are dancing with emotions and emotions are leading and expectations are waning, strength is being stolen. Stability is being shaken. I am raising up a company of women, an army of My powerful daughters, who walk upon the water with Me. They live in a place of the impossible becoming possible, their hearts bursting with "nothing is impossible for those who believe" faith, because they live being led by My Spirit and on the foundational truths of My Word. They are bold. They are fearless. They know their authority, and they live in and from a well of deep, hope-filled expectancy because they are drinking deeply from the never-ending water of My Word and My Spirit, not the well of emotions that runs dry.*

His voice continued to surround me:

*You must live saturated. The key to living in a place where you worship Me with your expectations and are full of expectant faith-filled hope is that you must live saturated. Saturated in My Word is that My presence and living always before My face. Many have become tired and looked away, looked down at circumstances and looked around at the natural realm. Fixed. Locked gaze. Eye to eye. That is the place you will remain.*

I could feel the alignment of the Lord. I could feel His powerful hand bringing forth divine order, and in the alignment of the Lord, there was great strength.

Again His voice surrounded me:

*Lana, great strength will be needed for the days ahead for My people, and they have all the strength given to them that is found in Me. I AM their strength. My Bride is swiftly moving into the days of being further acquainted with who I am as the GREAT I AM. But while many are living and dancing with emotions and tantalized with distraction, strength is stolen and taken. I am inviting My people deeper into the place of worshipping Me with their expectations. I am asking My people, "Do your expectations bring glory to Me and worship Me? Stop looking around you! Look up! Look up! It's time to look up! Look up higher. Make room! Make room! Make room! Ascend in your expectations, make room! There's more, there's more, there's more.*

As the Lord is raising up women of God living fully alive, He is fortifying His daughters in their foundation in Him and their expectations and that deep heart surgery that is taking place is removing those fractures. One of the fractures the Lord showed me was the word *floundering.*

As I leaned in and listened, I heard the Lord say, *"Many are floundering between two opinions. I am calling My people to* ***decide and*** *be* ***done*** *with doublemindedness, it's time to decide.* ***Time to decide."***

The sense filled the atmosphere of declaring and deciding to stand in who He is and who the Word says He is and worship Him with our expectations. There was a *resolve* in expectation that the Lord was calling His people to, and the positioning was in the *beholding* of who He is and refusing to look at anything else. Nothing else but Jesus.

To live as a woman of God fully alive, is to live as a woman who beholds Him face to face, ministering to Him—and from that place we live *decided.* Every day we live *decided* in His goodness, His truth, His power, His love; and when expectations arise that do not glorify the Lord, instead of giving them airplay, we look deeper into His eyes, *decided* that all that is within Him is good, all His thoughts toward us are good, and His Word and His truth have the final say.

## Abound in Him

The Lord's heart is for you to abound in freedom and wholeness and to abound in expectation. Heavenly expectation. I want you to think about that for a moment. Think about the word *abound.*

What pictures come to mind thinking of the word *abound?* Abound does not speak of little or just enough. Google defines *abound* as "to exist in large numbers or amounts," and synonyms of *abound* include "to thrive, to flourish, to lavish, superabundant, ample, plentiful, generous, inexhaustible, boundless." And that's just to name some of the synonyms.

So think about that, the Lord's heart for you is to thrive, flourish, live in superabundance, plentiful, inexhaustible, boundless expectations. Why? Because HE is the God of abundance. He is the Ephesians 3:20 God. He is the God of more than enough. David says in Psalm 23:5 (AMP), "*You prepare a table before me in the presence of my enemies. You have anointed and refreshed my head with oil. My cup overflows.*" He is the abundant God who loves to lavish and overflow blessing, love, grace, and peace into the lives of His people. He is the abundant Father who sent His One and only Son Jesus to die in our place so we could be reconciled unto Him, forgiven of sin, and have everlasting life. Living in *abundant* life (John 10:10).

As we look at just a few of those biblical truths and we see how abundant the Lord is and how beautiful and loving He is, as we see what is ours in Christ Jesus, the more we are rooted in Him—and in these truths, abiding deeply, our expectations *flourish*.

There is a tidal wave of the Refiner's fire, and it is flowing all through the body of Christ. As we behold Him as His people, His fire falls upon us and completely consumes the expectations that are not glorifying the Lord and ignites the fire of faith within hearts. There is a complete reversal taking place. A total turnaround. A divine alignment of the Lord and divine order comes into hearts and minds, shifting and changing our sight as we behold Him.

## Outpouring

The Lord is calling us as His daughters to a place of greater stewardship of our expectations before Him. As we are aligning our hearts in expectant faith before the Lord and allowing the Refiner's fire to purify, we are making room for *outpouring*.

I heard those words over and over, "*Alignment makes room for outpouring.*"

As we cry out for the fire of God upon our expectations, a birthing of hunger takes place. There is a groaning, a deep cry being birthed within His daughters and increased within us for more of Him—to know Him more, hear Him more, see Him more, and to experience a powerful move of His Spirit in our midst.

Daughter of God, woman of God, we are being called by the Lord to anchor more deeply within His Word and make room for Him in our expectation. It's time for the Bride to arise in faith in greater ways and take Him at His Word and to not flounder, but to stand fortified. There's a deeper consecration that the Lord is bringing His people into. A consecration unto Him as He is about to do wonders among us (Joshua 3:5).

The shaking upon expectations is uprooting expectations that are rooted in past hurts, past seasons, trauma, grief, and circumstances; how things have happened before, they are all coming out. Daughter of God, hear this truth. He is bringing things up to bring them out. He is bringing you further into the wholeness that is already yours in Christ. As you embrace the fire, as you embrace the heart surgery of the Lord upon your expectations in the place of abiding and deep intimacy, He is setting you free from things that have held you down, making room for the outpouring of His Spirit to increase your faith.

I see there are fresh and deep encounters with Jesus for you in this space. I see the words *exponential expectations*. He is bringing you into a place of living in a supernatural realm of *exponential expectations*.

I can hear your heart saying, "That would take a miracle," and you're absolutely right, because it will be a miracle. A powerful move of His Spirit that is not only going to restore your hope, restore expectations, and restore faith, but the fire of His love and the beauty of His face are going to usher you into a whole other world of expectation—and it's not an expectation that you can conjure up in your own strength. It's an expectation that flourishes from the place of beholding Him, abiding in Him, *being* with Him.

Your eyes are going to come alive in His presence more and more in this new era as you behold Him. Your eyes that have felt dim and heavy from fatigue of past seasons are going to be full of life as you look at the One who is *Life* itself. The Giver of life. The very Source of life. Heavenly vision is being restored to you to *see* on a level you have not seen before. Not just to see the promises contained in the Word and grab hold of them, but to see God's plans for your life, your family's life, and your city and nation on a scale you have never seen. The weight of sadness, heaviness, hope deferred, disappointments, pain, trauma, and all the effects of the past seasons that have affected your divine sight, insight, and expectation are being burned and washed away in His presence.

## A New Era

This isn't just a new day, it's a new era. I hear the Lord saying,

> *The place of feeling like you need to constantly fight to remain in expectation, I am now bringing you up higher as you abide in Me, to a place of living in the* **overflow** *of expectation in Me that does not have* **anything** *to do with the natural realm. It's founded in* **Me, the great I AM.**

There is whole new level of warfare worship that you are entering into as you step deeper into the awakening revelation that your expectations bring glory to Him, that faith-filled expectation brings glory and worships Him, and there is no room for anything else.

There is a whole new level of awakening the Lord is leading you into to understand that as you live in expectant hope and faith in who He is and the power of His Word, the demonstration of His power and His faithfulness, as you abide in Him and nestle deeply into His heart, pushes out anything that tries to stand against the expectation of His nature and His Word and makes room for an outpouring of His Spirit.

And think about this, how it moves His heart to see your expectations align with Him and His truth. We know that Hebrews 11:6 (TPT) says, *"And without faith living within us it would be impossible to please God. For we come to God in faith knowing that he is real and that he rewards the faith of those who passionately seek him."*

When we put our expectations and faith in Him, oh the joy and delight it brings to His heart, how it ministers to Him. The joyful aroma that it brings to His heart when we lift our eyes in expectancy of Jesus to move and to do what He said He was going to do, to finish what He started; oh the joy and pleasure it brings to Him.

Remember, you do not do this alone. He is your ever present help in time of need (Psalm 46:1) and in those moments, when you and I are desperately in need of Him to help us in stewarding our expectations, *ask Him.* He does not push you to the side and condemn you, He empowers you, ministers to you, reveals Himself to you again, and strengthens you with *His* faith to live a decided life, not a divided life.

It's a lifelong journey of growing up into expectancy. Heavenly expectancy. Living from our heavenly seat. Living the ascended life in our expectations that worships and glorifies Him. Oh Lord, refine our expectations as we behold You. As we abide, Refiner's fire, continue to purify our expectations and help us to steward our expectations well in the light of Your presence as we continue to behold You, the great I AM, the God of *more* than enough, our *abounding,* glorious, beautiful God.

Let our expectations sing a song of worship to You.

Daughter of God, be still, listen to the song of worship that your expectations sing to Him as you continue to grow up into living as a woman of God, fully alive, whose heart expectations minister to Him.

I'm with you in the "growing up process."

# 8

# HE IS REDEEMING THE FORFEITED GROUNDS OF YOUR LIFE

Have you ever had those moments in your life when the Lord shows you grounds of your life that you have forfeited and you hadn't even realized that you had? Those moments when the revelation hits hard and all of a sudden you realize that you've let go of things that you were meant to occupy and steward?

Well yep, that happened to me recently. The Lord began to show me "grounds" of my life that I had forfeited and I didn't even realize. I sat in this realization with the Lord, that I had let go and dropped some things that the Lord had said were mine to occupy. I had been through (and continue to go through) a fire upon my expectations and how my expectations had been affected by the seasons I had walked, and now the Lord showed me the grounds I had forfeited. Wow! My heart was bursting with repentance again, but expectation and excitement began to bubble in me, because if the Lord was bringing these things into the light, they were about to be dealt with, and I was going to occupy afresh.

So as my heart was in a deep place of repentance and I could feel the stirrings of expectation and excitement to occupy afresh, suddenly I felt a righteous indignation at the relentless battle that had been waged over these grounds of my life that I was called to occupy. A fresh conviction and passion started to be ignited within me for these lands and grounds I was called to stand in.

I began to realize more and more that in places where the enemy had come after these areas, where my heart had grown tired in these areas, where life had just become so intense and overwhelming, there was one thing that was majorly affected and pushed against in my life, in all of these different areas, and do you know what it was?

It was my authority!

## Standing in Authority

All of this affected my authority; the weariness I faced (both natural and spiritual) screamed at me to "just lie down, it's too hard, give up." Now let me pause here for a second. I believe it is really important that in every season we ask the Lord what our posture is to be: "Lord, do I fight right now? Or is it a season when I stand still and watch You fight for me?" (Exodus 14:14). I really have learned how important it is to discern the posture of the season.

There is a very deep and powerful place of "standing" and watching the Lord fight for you and resting in that. And there is a very deep and powerful place where the Lord says, "Run head-on into battle and fight." What I realized is, in both postures I am standing in authority.

As I stand still and watch the Lord fight for me, I am standing in His authority, resting, knowing that He is fighting for me and I am an overcomer, so I can let go, exhale and allow the Lord to fight for me, knowing He has assured my victory. My posture is not one of "lying down and giving up" but of "resting and allowing Him to fight for me." There's a very big difference and that difference is in my belief system, my heart posture and expectancy. I am standing in authority because I am standing in His authority and watching Him fight for me.

Then in the seasons when He says, "Run head-on into battle and fight," I am not running from a place of my own strength—I am armed with strategy from the Lord and the Word of God and allowing the Spirit of God to empower me and the Word to accomplish what I have been sent to do as I align my faith with what He has spoken. As I pray, as I intercede, as I pray in the Spirit, I am doing so from a place of His authority and recognizing that I am simply enforcing what Christ has already done and standing in it. I am not out there wielding my sword here, there, and everywhere, and fighting in my own strength and my own way. No. I am standing in a place of ferocious faith to see the Lord overcome, because He has overcome and I overcome in Him.

**Posture is important!**

So back to my process of being shown how I had forfeited grounds in my life. My "lying down" was not from a place of rest, believe me. As the Lord shone His light upon the areas where I had forfeited ground and my authority had been abdicated or I had stepped out of it, you know what His light brought into view? Fear!

I had given fear a voice. A very loud voice in my life. I had forfeited the grounds that the Lord had called me to occupy and to steward because I had become fearful. Fearful of more battle, more warfare, fearful of even being "seen" because the lies had come against me for so long, bombarding my mind and my heart to attempt to convince me that what I was carrying or what I was hearing was wrong.

Let me tell you, now that the Lord has brought this into the light, I can see so clearly what the enemy was trying to do. He was not only trying to stop me from occupying and moving with the Lord in all my assignments, but there was a deeper reason that the enemy was coming against me and it actually had nothing to do with me, really. He wanted and wants to stop the move of God on earth. I am just one of the vessels in the body of Christ the Lord is using to extend His Kingdom. I think in the Church today we have made an idol out of "destiny" and out of "our destiny." Our one purpose is to know Him and to know His heart deeply and go into all the world and preach the gospel. He is always the focus, not me. Not us.

So it struck me at an even deeper level. The enemy was after me and the ground that the Lord has called me to occupy because the enemy wants to hinder and stop the move of God and His voice going forth. So if the enemy is after stopping the move of God in my life, it is God He is trying to stop and God will not be stopped. Almighty God has already overcome and He is victorious. So when I am faced with grounds I am called to occupy being attempted to be taken from me, I can stand with a strong conviction that the Lord will not be stopped. This truth doesn't negate my responsibility to obey, show up, and steward well—it concretes a heart posture of victory.

## Ascend and Apprehend

As I sat with the Lord and sought His heart in the areas where I had forfeited, these areas I had abandoned, He spoke:

> *I am redeeming these places, and I am turning the forfeited places to the fortified places; and these places where the enemy has attempted to chase you out, now he will be evicted from these territories through the fire of My presence that shall inhabit these spaces and places. My Refiner's fire has purified you, has strengthened you, has purged you, has brought to the surface the hidden places of fear, and I have consumed them. I am now consuming you afresh with the fire of My*

> *presence. Your mouth shall be filled with the fire of My Word and the fire of My heart and love, and your eyes shall see the mysteries and wisdom contained in My Word and the secrets hidden deeply within My heart for you to pursue and receive. In the redeeming, there is a place of intentionality that you must step deeper into. It's the place of apprehending. It's the place of apprehending the land that I have spoken to you to occupy and to apprehend the enemy from being able to take these places from you any longer. It is time to ascend and apprehend.*

The word *apprehend* was so loud in my spirit as He spoke, so I grabbed my dictionary: APPREHEND: "To arrest someone for a crime" (synonyms: to arrest, catch, capture, seize, take prisoner, detain, nab, imprison). "To understand or perceive," "to seize either physically or mentally" (synonyms: comprehend, to realize, to recognize, to appreciate, to discern, to penetrate, to grasp, to fathom).

I could feel the call of the Lord strongly. His invitation to apprehend was so strong, it required a strong response.

The intensity of the invitation and call for intense response reminded me of Matthew 11:12:

> *From the days of John the Baptist until now the kingdom of heaven suffers violent assault, and violent men seize it by force [as a precious prize]* (AMP).

> *From the moment John stepped onto the scene until now, the realm of heaven's kingdom is bursting forth, and passionate people have taken hold of its power* (TPT).

It was a call to decide and to guard. It was a call to be ferocious in the apprehension and make the decision to not only take back the ground that had been forfeited but to come up higher in divine wisdom and heavenly strategy to see and watch over the areas where the enemy was trying to invade and lead me to forfeit.

I was struck by the intensity of the invitation of the Lord and struck by the realization that I hadn't even realized that I had forfeited those grounds He had called me to steward and occupy.

The Lord spoke again: "It is time for you to come up higher and ascend in your gatekeeping and your watching over."

It was time to come up higher. I could hear the sound of victory in the Spirit as the Lord raises up His daughters in greater ability to discern what He is saying, uncover the plans of the enemy, and enforce the victory of Christ in the grounds and spaces that He has called them to occupy. I was flooded with images of women all around the world who were given assignments of the Lord and the territories they were to occupy and they were feeling like they were constantly living in battle mode to stay in these places and maintain the ground that they had. That constant battle mode had brought them to a halt or caused them to feel like they were barely surviving in these spaces—but now the tide has turned.

The Lord detoxed them from the human systems built upon things not of the Lord. The Lord had refined the spaces that needed refining, and the Lord had uprooted the fears that contained them and continued to uncover areas where the enemy had targeted them and laid blame upon them. When in actual fact, all along it was the onslaught of the enemy bringing false accusations and whispering, "There's something wrong with you" so deeply in their hearts that they were constantly feeling as if they were living under everything. Feeling as if there was another area of the heart to deal with or another open door to close. There were definitely things the Lord has revealed and dealt with in this season in the heart and areas of open doors, but the enemy had laid blame by tempting many women to fight the wrong battles.

The Lord showed me that what you may have been facing is not a result of brokenness within you. You may have been tormented by thoughts that you are so broken that no matter how much you search within you, you cannot seem to find the breakthrough, the thing to release you from this onslaught in the grounds you are called to occupy. This is a demonic onslaught that has come against you to convince you that there is something deeply wrong with you, brokenness within you, and to keep you in a place of feeling like a victim, feeling like you are never going to come up and out into wholeness and truly begin to move into the space that He is calling you into—the place of governing.

We are in the era of exposure. The Lord is exposing, He is uncovering and bringing the hidden things into the light. The Refiner's fire has been hot and the Lord is healing His people and bringing us further and further into wholeness. There is a mighty deliverance happening in the body of Christ right now. Hallelujah!

But, you may have taken the evil one's bait. You may have taken the blame. You may have turned your eyes away from thinking it could be a demonic onslaught from a fear of "overspiritualizing" and you have turned your eyes completely upon your own heart to find the problem within you. The enemy is trying to lure you into agreement.

Let me remind you—as you sit deeply in the secret place, close to His heart—He will expose, uncover, convict, reveal, and deal with what needs to be dealt with in your heart as you stay tender, open, surrendered, and listening to Him.

But the enemy has caused you to lay down your sword. I heard the Lord say it:

> *The enemy has caused you to lay down your sword, by turning your eyes to your own heart. I say unto you to lift up your eyes and pick up your sword again and speak My Word against the enemy. Arise and speak. Rebuke and bind. Take*

> *back the authority that is yours. It is time for you, warrior woman, to arise and take your place of authority back again. It's time for you to not only occupy the ground and the spaces He has called you to, but to govern in these places.*

I prophesy to you, daughter of God, as you pick up your sword again and stare down the giants in your land that have driven you out, declare the Word of God by faith and stand strong upon the Word. As you stand on the living, active, alive Word of God (Ephesians 6) and you speak, declare, and pray the Word, you will see the Lord drive the enemy out of your land and redeem your ground. Then you will be positioned in Him to govern in these spaces.

There is a realm of divine intel, wisdom, and discernment that the Lord is leading you into. The stretching and the battle has exposed the need for greater discernment and wisdom in this hour. I see this realm is available to you in greater measure than you have walked in before. Divine strategies, innovations, the wisdom of Heaven, and divine intelligence are awaiting you, and you will be moving in these spaces the Lord has called you to occupy with governance in this hour. You will begin to see the move of the Spirit in these places begin to carry the wisdom and intelligence of the Lord into the nations. You will begin to see the glory of the Lord and the power of His Spirit go forth from these places that He has called to, to establish His Kingdom and manifest His glory on earth.

I see that as you stay tender before the Lord in these areas you are called to occupy—to lean in and listen and remain ferocious in your apprehending what He is offering you—there is a mighty habitation of His glory in your midst. There is a mighty habitation of His heart and His presence that will invade these spaces and territories that He has called you to occupy, and you will see many come and hear and see, from near and far, what the Lord is doing in your midst.

The glory of the Lord will be visible from your home and many will be drawn to the light of Jesus. The fire of His presence will blaze in your prayer room, and the fire of God will be visible for people to see and be drawn to. There is a realm of the miraculous that awaits you in this hour, and it is not from a heart that is seeking out miracles, but from the heart of one who is a laid-down lover of Jesus who has recognized the door is in the floor. This realm is to go deeper and deeper still in humility and surrender with a fierce resolve to stand hand in hand, shoulder to shoulder with the Avenger, the beautiful Jesus, the Beloved Lord, the Lion of Judah, and not move from where He has called you to occupy.

I hear Him saying:

> *Show up! Show up! Show up! There has been a showdown in these areas I have called you to occupy, but I have and am showing Myself strong in your midst as you stand and apprehend. Show up again in the spaces you forfeited. Show up again in the places that were taken from you and know that you are not staying where you are. In the spirit, things are constantly moving and you are not only taking back the ground that the enemy has taken, but you are now moving forward with Me into a whole new realm of divine mystery, spiritual wisdom and understanding, and expansion of territory. A place where you host My heart and host My glory. A hub of transformation. An ark of My glory. Watch as these battlegrounds now turn to war rooms where I release My divine strategy and intel to you, to govern with Me, moving from feeling like a victim to victor, from defense to offense.*
>
> *I am calling you to show up! I am calling you forth. I am calling you to the frontline. I am calling you back into the places I have anointed you to move in. I am calling you to the*

*pioneering pathways I have for you in this hour. I am calling you forth, warrior woman. I am calling you into new realms of divine intel. I am calling you to SHOW UP again.*

*Watch now, as you show up again...*

*I will show up!*

# 9

# REMAIN FAITHFUL TO THE VISION GOD HAS GIVEN YOU

Daughter of God, I hear the Lord say, "*Remain faithful to the vision I have given you.*"

My heart in this chapter is to bring forth encouragement to those who have been carrying a vision and strategies for a long time and to encourage you to remain steadfast and faithful to what He has given you. I also bring forth encouragement to those waiting on the vision and strategies of God, and I release prophetic insight for you to posture yourself to remain faithful to the new visions and strategies coming to you in this new era.

So, come sit with me and let's have a chat.

Have you ever found yourself in a season when it feels like you have been given a vision from God and you feel like Noah? You're building an ark because God told you to and rain is coming (back then, whatever in the world is rain?!). And some people just don't understand or they are certainly not running alongside you in your vision. Instead of cheers of celebration and encouragement, you're hearing and feeling an atmosphere full of "You're crazy! What are you doing? That's too out of the box. That's not the way it's done," and on and on the comments go.

But you know, that you know, that you know that the Lord has spoken to you.

In this new era, the Lord is raising up His daughters who will "mother movements." I want you to understand that today. The vision God has given you is bigger than you. There has been warfare and opposition over the vision, and at some points you have felt like carrying the vision will almost kill you.

**But God!**

He has sustained you, He continues to empower you, and He continues to strengthen you to carry the vision and implement the vision. Like Nehemiah, you cannot be distracted and come down off the wall (see Nehemiah 6). You must continue to build what the Lord has called you to build.

Daughter of God, precious woman, maybe part of your story is that you feel misunderstood. You have taken a stand and been rejected, or you have followed the strategies and visions He has given you and you feel like a misfit or you don't fit in—or maybe you've been labeled "wrong" by others or you have labeled yourself as "wrong."

First, I want you to know that you are *not* wrong. I want to suggest to you, could you be pioneering something new, the new thing God is doing? You have been carrying the heart of God, the expression of God, the creativity of God, vision of God, and the revelation of God that many in your circle were not ready to hear. It is a lie of the enemy that has labeled you that you are wrong and what you carry is wrong. The enemy has used this label to cause you to hide and try to wear you down; but daughter of God, oh the excitement in my spirit to encourage you and tell you that in this hour more than *ever* before you are going to experience the Lord bringing you into context. You are going to experience the

Lord bring you out of deep condemnation for the wrestle of feeling wrong that you have lived in for so many years of your life. There is a fierceness and expression of His Spirit within you that has burned so deeply in you, that at times you have apologized for, that I have spoken about quite a lot in this book, but it is no more. The Lord is bringing you into context for such a time as this.

The Lord has seen your tears. The Lord has seen the years of pain, the Lord has seen the rejection. The Lord has seen the negative words spoken over you and who you are and what you carry; but daughter of God, precious woman of God, fellow sister in Christ, the Lord is healing you. The Lord is delivering you. The Lord is setting you free. The Lord is igniting you more and more with His fire and increasing the fire within you, for this is your great revealing where you shall reveal and shine His glory in ways you have never seen. You shall carry forth His fire that will activate, ignite, and bring the fire of His presence, the hammer of His Word, the fire of His conviction, and the passionate love of God through you in unprecedented ways.

Daughter of God, listen to me, where you have faced great injustice, the Lord is healing you, setting you free, bringing you recompense and restoration, and recommissioning you where the injustice took you out of some of what the Lord has called you to do. Not only is the Lord setting those things right, He is anointing you to go forth to see *His justice* released through your prayers, your decrees, your voice, and new assignments the Lord will place in your hands.

Where you have endured the brunt of injustice, this is the hour when you will see the recompense and manifested justice in your life. Watch and see much of what the Lord has spoken to you and imparted to you and placed within you that you have felt at times you have not understood, or has not fit, or made you feel like a misfit, *now* come into context. There has been a forerunning the Lord may have had you walking in that you have not even realized or understood, but now you will.

## No Longer a Misfit

I hear the Lord speaking over you, precious daughter:

> *Where these precious daughters of mine have been rejected, labeled as misfits, many of them for all their lives and many of them for many years, I am saying you fit perfectly in My heart. You live deeply in My heart, and I am now sending you forth with a compass of My heart to reveal and guide My ways in this new era.*
>
> *Many have spoken over you* ***misfit****, but I am speaking* ***movement!*** *This is your time to* ***move, move, move*** *in fullness of the expression of My heart, My nature, My love, My creativity, and My blueprint* ***through you.*** *You are birthing a movement with Me. Living under the word "misfit" will be no longer. You are a wild one, a passionate one, created not to fit in but to stand out and to pioneer the uncharted terrains and unexplored pathways that will make room for My glory.*
>
> *The pathways that many have feared to tread because they have enjoyed the comfort of the familiar, the cost has been too high, or they fear going against the grain, you My wild one, were born to carve these pathways with Me and lead others into the new things that I am going to do, which are outside of all that they have known, and champion them with courage to follow Me wherever I lead, no matter the cost. My daughters, again, no longer living under a word "misfit" but now living under the word of partnering with* ***My movement.***
>
> *You were born to break the box! You were born to break the box! You have looked down upon yourself for the fire*

> *within you, but I placed the anointing upon you and the fire within you to break boxes that human wisdom and expectation have created. You were not born to live in a box. You were born to* ***break the boxes*** *through the expression of My heart, My love, and My fire through you. You are coming forth! You are coming forth My wild one! Bridled no longer! Free to run! Free to soar! This is your time to arise and shine and the King of Glory is coming* ***through you!*** *Run, wild one,* ***run!***

The Lord is dealing with all the things in your heart that hinder you from taking a stand in this hour as you embrace His Word and His fire. It's a new day, and the call to stand in the coming days is getting louder.

I had an encounter recently and I heard the Lord say, *"Be prepared in the coming days to stand and not compromise the blueprints I have given you."*

Where there have been things you may have endured for what you carry and the expression of Jesus through your life, your gifting, your fire, your creativity, etc., the Lord has healed and is healing. As the call to stand strong in the blueprints the Lord is releasing and not compromise on them is getting weightier, you can stand in this hour without compromise. Any doors or legal right of the enemy in your heart that causes you to shy away from all the Lord is calling you to stand in are eliminated by His healing hand.

In this encounter, I heard the Lord speaking: *"I am calling you deeper. Deeper and deeper into the secret place to know My heart and listen to My voice."*

Before we go on, can I remind you, ministry is not the focus. Ministry is not the priority. *Jesus* is the priority and seeking first the Kingdom of God (Matthew 6:33) is our priority. To know Him, that's our priority. To be known *by* Him and to know His heart and His ways. Deep intimacy, that's our priority. None of us want to be found in a place of Matthew 7:21-23 (ESV):

> *Not everyone who says to me "Lord, Lord" will enter the kingdom of heaven, but the one who does the will of my Father who is in heaven. On that day many will say to me, "Lord, Lord, did we not prophesy in your name, and cast out demons in your name, and do many mighty works in your name?" And then will I declare to them, "I never knew you; depart from me, you workers of lawlessness."*

Intimacy with Him is our priority, and I hear the heart of the Lord resounding and calling His Church deeper than ever into that place of deep, deep communion with Him.

Let's continue.

I want to share parts of a prophetic word the Lord gave me for the body of Christ here, because I believe there is such wisdom, insight, direction, and encouragement for us as His daughters in this hour to stand unapologetically, not compromising the blueprints He has given us.

I heard Him say:

> *For there are tests coming in the coming days in this season when you, My people, will see pressures coming in many directions upon the new blueprints that I am calling you to build with Me, that you will have to stand against. The empowerment, the courage, and the boldness needed to stand against these pressures that will come against you for moving in obedience to Me—especially when it looks out of the box and challenges others' complacency—will be the foundation of the secret place with Me. There will be so much grace*

*upon the new blueprints that I am releasing and calling you to build and pioneer with Me on earth, but those who are faint of heart and do not know Me deeply will find it hard to withstand the pressures that will come with the new things I am releasing and building.*

*My Refiner's fire has been intense and it has been hot, but I am returning for a pure and spotless Bride. I am going deep into all areas where there is compromise in the hearts and lives of My people as I am raising up an army who will stand uncompromisingly for My truth and My ways in the coming days. Those who will not bow to other gods, man-made ways, or pressures in these days. There are many who have not been embracing My Refiner's fire, yet I continue to call out and I continue to knock at the doors of their hearts to call them back to Me and call them back into union with Me, but many refuse to open the door of their hearts (Revelation 3:20). When the time comes for them to stand for Me in the ways that I am leading that are out of the box, not what they have known before, and are against the crowd, they will not be able to stand because they have compromises within their hearts.*

*I am calling My people back to Myself, and I am not raising up an army that falls down weakly to pressures and whatever comes their way. I am raising up an army that lives in deep union with Me; in deep intimacy they know Me and are deeply founded on My Word. They stand in Me and for Me, no matter the cost. I have been dealing with the compromises in the hearts of those embracing My Refiner's fire in these days, so My army will arise* ***uncompromisingly strong and unapologetic.***

*There has been much toxic poison festering beneath the surface in many hidden places in the body of Christ, and it is not only displeasing to Me, it has cultivated a compromising Church. I did not die and give My life for My Church to walk in ways of compromise and be a compromising Church. I paid a great price for a Church of laid-down lovers who live in deep intimacy with Me and know Me and follow Me, uncompromisingly and unapologetically.*

*There is also going to be an increase in tests regarding the blueprints I release that will require great uprooting and a no-toleration stand. For there are specific instructions I will release that will highlight areas where you will have to partner with Me to see My Spirit* ***uproot*** *what does not belong, and you must obey and follow My leading. There are also areas where I am exposing. As I release these new blueprints, great insight and discernment will accompany these blueprints that I will give to you, that will specifically unveil the spirit of Jezebel and where she has been hidden in many places. As you follow Me and My instructions, she will be confronted, uprooted, and brought down by My power and My name—but you* ***must*** *follow My instructions and you must* ***not*** *tolerate her. For in these days I am exposing and uncovering those who have tolerated Jezebel; and where she has been given free rein and access, I am calling for repentance.*

*My people, do not allow the enemy to come into your ears in the coming days and try to convince you that the blueprints I give to you are wrong because of the confrontation they bring or expose. For I am separating, exposing, uncovering, and bringing deliverance—watch the spirit of Elijah come like never before. I am bringing down all that is not founded in Me or what is a mixture; these new blueprints, as they are obeyed and followed, will challenge what is not founded in intimacy, purity, and My ways.*

*There will be great temptation in the coming days to compromise the instructions that I give to you, My people. I am releasing a warning to you to stay deeply in the place of intercession. For in the place of intercession you will find great strength in Me, and intercession will release the instructions that I have for you for each step and to move where you need to move. Many have felt they have been living under the fog of witchcraft and unable to see clearly, but I am causing you ascend above where you shall see in ways that you have not seen before.*

*There will be an even greater dying to people's applause and reputation that will take place in the coming days for many to follow Me and My ways and to build in the way I am calling you to build with Me. Do not be counted in this hour as one who lives in compromise or compromises the blueprints and instructions that I give to you. Come deeper into the secret place with Me and know Me, for the temptation to cut corners and compromise in the coming days will be great—but those who have died to self and continue to live in a place of deep surrender to Me will arise to build the arks that will host My glory.*

*There is great cost to follow Me, and in the coming days there will be greater cost in following Me. The blueprints that I am releasing will pioneer in new ways with Me; the glory that you shall see in your midst and the power of My Spirit that shall flow will be unprecedented. The provision and miracles in your midst as you follow Me in obedience from the place of deep intimacy and knowing Me will be something that you have never experienced before.*

Daughter of God, woman of God living fully alive, I call you forth to live fully alive as you live in deep intimacy with Him and know Him and His ways. As you yield to Him and His ways and His fire, answering the call to be *all in* in this hour, you are going to see in greater ways how He has prepared you for these days. You will see how He is preparing you for these times to come.

As you live close to His heart, you will hear His instruction. As you live in the place of intercession, you will receive the insight needed to build according to the blueprint and strategy of the Lord for your life in this new era. This is the time when you are coming into context.

## Fierce Determination

I charge you in this hour, daughter of God, to arise in boldness and courage. Arise again in fierce determination to allow the Holy Spirit to have His way in your heart and in your life, whatever the cost. I pray a fresh baptism of fire over you in this hour, that you will be consumed afresh by the fiery presence and power of the Lord. That His fierce and ferocious eyes of fire would overtake you again.

Arise, uncompromising daughter! Arise in this hour, shaking off and leaving behind all that has hindered you. No longer look back—look to Jesus, look forward into all He is leading you into. I encourage you to give your whole life to Him afresh today, throw yourself again upon the altar and watch His fire fall upon your life.

*Beloved friends, what should be our proper response to God's marvelous mercies? To surrender yourselves to God to be his sacred, living sacrifices. And live in holiness,*

> *experiencing all that delights his heart. For this becomes your genuine expression of worship. Stop imitating the ideals and opinions of the culture around you, but be inwardly transformed by the Holy Spirit through a total reformation of how you think. This will empower you to discern God's will as you live a beautiful life, satisfying and perfect in His eyes* (Romans 12:1-2 TPT).

Sometimes in our journey of carrying a vision that the Lord has given us, we can often find ourselves being pulled in different directions and tempted to compromise the vision, shift the vision, or adjust the vision so that it fits with "what is normally done" or according to "what others think."

Sometimes we find ourselves in such a battle over carrying the Lord's strategy or blueprint—especially when it is unfamiliar to what we have moved in before, how we have built, or where He has led us—that we need to become deeply rooted in His nature, His way, and move forward with our trust completely in Him and how He is leading us. Sometimes obedience to the Lord leads us in directions that we never thought we would walk in, and stepping out of the boat sometimes is a lot scarier than we thought. But I believe in this hour the Lord is raising up His daughters who are living in deeper and deeper levels of trusting Him and following Him wherever He leads. It is a place where fear of man must die. You cannot carry the new thing that the Lord has given you and walk in it in obedience and boldness if you're caught in the fear of man. Can I invite you right now to lay down the fear of man before the Lord if that's something you're struggling with. Bring it before the Lord and repent for aligning with it, and ask the Lord to come and minister to you and break it off of your life.

Looking at the life of Jesus, He never diverted from the strategy and will of the Father. He remained faithful to His assignment, even to the point of death (Philippians 2:8). When Peter rebukes Jesus after Jesus tells them that He must be killed and on the third day be raised to life (Matthew 16:21), Jesus turns and rebukes Peter, saying, *"Get behind me, Satan! You are a stumbling block to me; you do not have in mind the concerns of God, but merely human concerns"* (Matthew 16:23 NIV). Jesus then goes on in verses 24-28 to tell His disciples that whoever wants to be His disciple must take up their cross and follow Him and lose their life in order to find it.

There is a call in this hour, daughter of God, to follow His vision, His strategies, His way, in a weightier way than I have ever felt it before. Whatever God is calling you to do, to build, to walk in, remain faithful to what He has called you to.

The Lord wants to minister to your heart and deliver you from anything that would hinder you from remaining faithful to His vision, His strategies in your life; and at the same time, there is a call from the heart of the Lord to follow Him whatever it looks like. He wants you to *not* be caught up in human concerns or in your own human understanding but to be a daughter who is continually pressing into Him more and more deeply to have the concerns of God ever before you.

There is such a freedom found in this truth here, daughter of God; the grace and the empowerment of His Spirit that carries you has gone before you and goes with you to remain faithful to the vision and His strategies and do what He has called you to do. This comes not from your own human effort, but from a deep trusting in Him, holding His hand and knowing that it is in and through Him (Acts 17:28) and by the power of His Spirit (Zechariah 4:6) that He does it through you. It's in the beautiful deep place of intimacy with Jesus and in surrender and obedience that you will find your greatest strength to remain.

There have been many times over the past few years when the temptation has been loud to me to "not remain." The battle has been fierce, it has felt like the price has been so high, the ground has been so hard to toil at times, but you know what has kept me? Not my own strength (thank God!), not my own ability (thank You Jesus!)—my love for Him is what has driven me. My love for Him to see every part of my life worship Him, bring glory to Him, minister to Him, and see the Lamb receive the reward of His suffering. Oh how He has kept me day after day after day after day. His constant encouragement, His beautiful presence, His words of truth, and His empowerment—it's all from Him and it's all for Him. I have a responsibility in my yes to Him and my obedience to Him, and He being my great reward, nothing else compares.

In closing, I want to share an encounter I had with the Lord recently, because as you chase after Him and keep your eyes on Him, He is solidifying the strategies and vision He has given you.

In this encounter, I heard the Lord say, *"I am solidifying My strategies."*

When the Lord spoke these words, I saw what looked like whirlwinds surrounding many people, whirlwinds of confusion that were blowing and roaring loudly, and I knew that they had been sent from the enemy to cause unrest and angst.

When I saw the word *angst,* this word was deeply highlighted to me: ANGST: A feeling of deep anxiety or dread. SYNONYMNS: anxiety, fear, dread, apprehension, worry, foreboding, trepidation, malaise, distress, disquiet, unease, uneasiness (Google).

These whirlwinds had come so suddenly into the lives of many believers. I knew that the whirlwinds came with a strategic accident to bring angst into the lives of believers. The *angst* was gaining entry through the *agreement* of the saints with its likes and its false narrative.

## Armed with Strength to Stand

Then God said:

> *These whirlwinds have come to bring deep unrest and angst in the lives of many in this hour, as the enemy is attempting*

*to oppose the* ***solidifying of My strategies*** *that I am releasing into the lives of My people. I am bringing My people into such a deep realm of* ***faith rest*** *in My strategies in this hour that they will* ***not*** *be shaken.*

*I say unto you, My people,* ***look not*** *to the whirlwinds. Lower your head between your knees like Elijah did (1 Kings 18) and remain in focused intercession on what I am speaking, the strategies I am releasing, and keep your eyes firmly focused upon Me. I say unto you, that as you continue to lift up your head to where your help comes from (Psalm 121) and you continue to keep your eyes firmly fixed upon Me (Hebrews 12:2) and you continue to* ***stand*** *upon the strategies that I am speaking and releasing in this hour, you are not only ascending into a greater realm of sitting in My counsel through your understanding of what I am speaking, but you are moving into a season of being the most solidified in My strategies. Not only am I solidifying My strategies within your lives with such clarity and confirmation, I am bringing forth a solidifying within you as I work deeply within your hearts to* ***remain steadfast,*** *standing upon the strategies that I am speaking in this hour.*

*My people, listen to Me, you are* ***not to move*** *from what I have spoken. You are* ***not*** *to move an inch from that which I have spoken. Now is the time to dig your heels in faith and stand ferociously upon the strategies that I am releasing to you in this hour: no matter what they look like, no matter the cost or the way, you* ***must remain.***

*I say unto you, that where the whirlwinds of the enemy has come to bring* ***angst****—as I am solidifying My strategies in your lives and you are remaining and standing upon that which*

*I have spoken—you will* ***see the winds of acceleration*** *upon these strategies, MY strategies, in ways you have not yet seen before. You will see the supernatural provision within My strategies, and the power of My Spirit will bring forth a mighty move of My Spirit through the strategies I am giving you in this hour that are unlike anything you have ever seen. But you* ***must*** *remain in faith, and there is a greater level of walking by faith and not by sight (2 Corinthians 5:7) in this hour.*

*My strategies in this hour will cause you to climb mountains you have never climbed and will cause you to pioneer paths and uncharted territories that you have never explored or imagined before. But as you remain steadfast upon the strategies I am releasing to you, you will see that it is not by might, nor by power, but by My Spirit (Zechariah 4:6).*

*My people, I say unto you, that for many of you in this hour this next-step strategy that I am releasing to you—as you step forth in obedience and remain steadfast upon that which I have spoken—this strategy that I have given you is going to open a* ***slipstream*** *of My Spirit that you have not experienced before. You will be carried in a level of grace that is unprecedented to you, and My Spirit will not only bring a great overcoming of the opposition of the enemy that has attempted to keep you from the land I am leading you into, but you will find a new level of My grace to build with Me in a significantly different way than you have known. It is going to require a new level of dependence upon Me as you learn to navigate new realms of alignments, community, and new ways of being led by Me in your building. Contained within My strategies is all the provision needed. Worry not about provision, for I have already gone before to provide all that is* *needed for you to build with Me in these new and unfamiliar, unprecedented ways.*

*I say unto you, where there has been an alignment with* **angst** *in this hour, come deeper, My people, and repent of angst. I am delivering you from* **angst** *in your repentance, and I am delivering your bodies from the effects of* **angst** *by the power of My Spirit and in the power of My name. I say unto you that I am turning the* **angst** *to* **anticipation** *in this hour, for the great and mighty works that I will do in your midst.*

*I say unto you that the whirlwinds have come strongly against you, but I am solidifying My strategies in your lives and I am bringing you deeper into the places of seeing Me do* **wonderous** *things among you. I am bringing you deeper into a place of seeing what you have never seen. Oh, how My strategies in this hour will lead you into deeper wonder of who I am and My power as you remain and obey. You have not imagined what I have planned. The strategies I am solidifying within you in this hour are much bigger than you realize. Watch what I will do through the strategies I am giving you in this hour, it is* **far beyond** *your comprehension. My glory will be revealed like you have not yet seen.*

*That is what the Scriptures mean when they say, "No eye has seen, no ear has heard, and no mind has imagined what God has prepared for those who love him" (1 Corinthians 2:9 NLT).*

Woman of God, can you feel the Lord's heart arming us in strength to stand and remain faithful to His vision and strategies He gives us in this hour? God is raising up women who are living fully alive, living fully solidified in the vision and strategies He is releasing to them. You are part of that company, daughter of God.

You go forth into the new assignments, not alone. He goes with you. As you answer the call, know that *all* you need to accomplish what He is asking you to is found in Christ and in His empowerment. He's just looking for your yes. No matter the cost to remain true to His blueprint, strategies and leadings in this hour, it compares not to the great reward that you receive for your obedience to Him.

*Him!*

His presence!

*He* is Your great reward.

Let's arise together in this hour, determined together that from the place of laid-down surrender and yielding to His fire, we arise as the uncompromising daughters of God, women of God fully alive in obedience to Him, that *will see* His glory come in and through our lives.

And daughter of God, let me remind you: It's not just visitations of His glory, but following His blueprints and instructions in complete obedience will see the winds of His Spirit accelerate all that He has for us. Watch the assignments that we shall put our hands to in humility and obedience to Him and see His Spirit take us into a realm of divine insight and spiritual understanding that we have not known. For this is the hour of His specific instruction and strategy; and where we have felt like strategy has been far from us and clouded by attacks of witchcraft, haze, and weariness, *now,* daughter of God, we shall know the divine intel of His heart, strategies, and wisdom from His Word like never before.

I hear Him say: "*You will see all you put your hands to be* ***terrains of transformation*** *as they become habitations of My glory.*"

Are you with me?

I'm all in!

# 10

# GOVERNING IN MOTHERING

"Governing in Mothering" is what I have titled this chapter because those are the words He spoke to me. I remember hearing those words and I remember feeling like I had been living so far below these words. To be honest, I realized that I was living as a victim in my mothering. No matter how hard I tried to position myself as a strong mother to lead my children in the ways of God, on the inside I felt like I was at war.

All. The. Time.

And the words *governing in mothering* exposed not only that victim space I had sat down in, in regard to my mothering, it exposed the war within me. Did I like that exposure? Absolutely not! Because part of my heart was exposed that was carrying some really deep pain that had drawn me down into what felt like a deep hole inside me, that no one saw, around my role as a mother.

I remember one night in the middle of the night having a dream and the Lord saying to me, "Lana, all the pain and disappointment you are carrying is about motherhood."

Ouch!

I woke up wishing He was wrong, but He wasn't, He never is! He was so right! So here I was, sitting with these words *governing in mothering* and feeling like my heart was full to the brim of pain and disappointment.

I realized in seasons gone by I had definitely been living in the realm of knowing what it looked like to govern in my mothering, but somehow over the past few seasons, things had begun to creep in, without me even realizing, leaving me in a place of such weariness in my mothering journey, but it was deeper than that. Things had slowly been etching away at my heart and how I saw myself as a mother that I had moved out of the place of truly governing how He was calling me to govern in my home, to a place of overwhelming confusion and feeling very lost.

All I could see was pain from relentless spiritual warfare against me as a mother, or against my family, my own belief systems that had shifted through looking at my own shortcomings, then walking through a season of multiple miscarriages; it was one thing after another. Little did I realize then that all those little things, when all piled up together, had slowly been draining the life out of my motherhood.

So I decided to sit quietly. I closed my eyes and allowed myself to look into my heart as a mother. There I found that pain and disappointment really quickly. What else did I find? I was holding myself to account. My very own heart was condemning me.

First John 3:20 (AMPC) filled my thoughts:

> *Whenever our hearts in [tormenting] self-accusation make us feel guilty and condemn us. [For we are in God's hands.] For He is above and greater than our consciences (our hearts), and He knows (perceives and understands) everything [nothing is hidden from Him].*

Golly, those words, "Whenever our hearts in tormenting self-accusation make us feel guilty and condemn us," hit me like a ton of bricks, right in the face of my mothering. In a moment, the Holy Spirit showed me that I had been living in such torment over my mothering because of the self-accusation I had been living in deep, deep, deep inside my heart. I began to see a stark reality.

I would never let myself off the hook.

I had never forgiven myself for all the mistakes and times when I thought I failed my kids. I had been living in such fear of "I don't want to damage my kids or see my kids live in brokenness and deep pain and torment from my parenting, like I did growing up."

So like a mouse on a wheel, my heart had been churning over and over and over, rehearsing all the mistakes, rehearsing all of the shortcomings and bottom line, rehearsing over and over what a terrible Mum I was. That was the statement:

"I am a terrible Mum."

And from there:

"I have damaged my kids and am damaging my kids."

So no matter how much someone might say to me, "You're such a great Mum, you're such an inspiration," it would bounce off a brick wall in my heart. I would politely smile and say, "Thank you," but there was no way my heart was receiving that, because my belief system, which told me I was a terrible Mum and had and was damaging my kids, ran really deep.

I tried to love and teach and lead my kids in the ways of the Lord, love them deeply, guide them, raise them to be amazing lovers and followers of Jesus, and I saw beautiful fruit in their lives. Then at times I saw the not-great fruit, the attitudes, the normal behavior in our children's lives that we have to navigate as parents. But instead of looking at those places and seeing them as places where I could come alongside them and lead them and teach them, I shut down. I found myself so confused; all of a sudden, I didn't know how to parent my children and lead them because I allowed some of the not-so-great fruit I was seeing in their lives outweigh the good fruit, and it screamed at me, "This is all your fault, look how you have failed them." This is not the environment where a mama can flourish.

I was caught in a cycle of deep unforgiveness and possibly even bordering on self-hatred for myself as a mother—and a huge, huge, huge place of regret.

Let me tell you, that's a heavy load for a heart to carry.

Governing in mothering began to expose all of these roots and belief systems in my heart that I was living with daily and was the filter through which I was parenting. I was faced with the stark reality that I had not forgiven myself even slightly; and if you came up and asked me for a list of all the ways I had wronged my kids, I could give it to you.

It was like I was living in this deep place of torment because I wanted to invest my whole heart to be Mum, that was my heart's desire, one of my greatest joys. But at the same time, I really struggled to be in that space because it kept reminding me so much of how much I was failing.

So governing in mothering not only exposed these areas, what I realized was it was not only an invitation into freedom and healing, it was also an invitation in redemption, restoration, and recompense. It was also an invitation into an ascended place of wisdom, health, and flourishing in my calling as a mother.

I felt stuck. Completely. Unable to move. No matter how much I would try to "faith my way out of" what I was feeling, I couldn't, because my heart was so shut down and locked into the lie of "I am a terrible mother." There was no way I was able to enter into the place of governing in my home when I was embracing and aligning with that statement.

I became really good at rehearsing that statement over and over and over again. I would sit with the Lord and ask the Lord to forgive me for believing that lie and for all the unforgiveness toward myself that had found a home in my heart and set up camp. But even though my prayers were to obey the Word of God and to lay it all at His feet, I felt my heart almost unwilling to budge because my warped belief system was so deep.

So I did all I knew to do, cry out to Jesus for help. Cry out to the Holy Spirit for help: "Jesus, break through my hardened, hurt, locked-away heart. Please step into these areas of my heart like only You can. Set me free from the torment I am living in and bring me back to life in my mothering."

## The Garden of My Heart

In the spirit I looked around at the garden of my heart in the area of mothering and you know what I saw? Barrenness. My belief system around my mothering had sucked all the life out of my mothering. My holding on to regret and pain was poisoning the garden of my heart. I was so deeply hiding in the area of mothering, I had never even realized it.

And these words, "From governing to mothering," were calling me out of hiding. Calling me higher and calling me to take my place again in my home as mother. Calling me into my role as mother from the place of how He sees me as mother.

That's when it hit me.

Governing in mothering is not given to me in my home from the Lord as something that I "earn" because I get everything right. Governing in mothering comes from Him, is in Him and through Him.

Here I have found myself trying to be the perfect mother, so then I can govern. Here I found myself not governing because of the "scorecard" I was keeping against myself. That scorecard had to be handed to Jesus, and that scorecard was immediately covered in His blood. He had it all covered. He was not holding a scorecard against me; He died so that there would be no scorecard held up against me. He died so I would be forgiven, reconciled, and covered by His grace and love.

Because He is the Source of governing, we haven't been given the authority to govern because we have got everything right, that's not what determines our governance, Jesus does. So when I think, What does it look like to live in the place of governing in mothering? I have to go back to the Source. Jesus!

As I sat, closed my eyes, and quieted my heart, I asked Jesus to speak to me, I felt Him so close, almost like I could feel His breath upon my ear. Then I heard a whisper: "Ask Me what I think of you as a mother."

I knew in that moment that I had entered the beginning of transformation. I knew I had come face to face with turnaround. With healing. With begin again. With restoration. With truly being set up to govern in my home like never before and how I was created to govern.

I knew that one question had the potential, if I asked it, to not only transform me but my legacy. I remember looking down at my hands, as if I was literally holding the question tangibly in my hands—and then all of a sudden, I had a vision and I saw it.

It was a sword.

Hearing what He had to say about me as a mother would become a weapon in my hands against the accusation—it was a sword to cut through the unbelief, the pain, the chains, the torment, the fear, the shame. It would not only sever it and cut through it, but it would open the way for healing to flow. A way for His balm and His love to flow in and bring healing to honestly, a very broken part of my heart.

It would make way for life.

It would make way for flourishing.

It would make way for a fortification in Him.

It would make way for joy.

It would make way for governing.

It would make way for fruitfulness.

It would make way for a move of His Spirit in me and through me, in greater increase.

I knew this moment would take great courage. It was accepting an invitation into deeper vulnerability with the Lord, to let Him truly see me (even though He knows me deeply to my innermost parts, He sees it all). To truly let Him "see me" was a call out of hiding into a place of courage to let the narrative be shifted and to sit in the uncomfortableness, at times, in the place of being deeply seen.

This was truly the first step to me learning all over again what it meant to live in the space of governing in mothering.

## "Ask Me"

I had to come back to the beginning and begin again with Jesus in this area. Sure my kids had grown up, years had gone by, but that whisper from Him, "Ask Me what I think of you as a mother," felt filled with the Lord's heart of restoration and a clean slate. My heart pondered: "Could this be a point where He restores all and nothing is wasted. Is this a new beginning for me as a mother? Could it begin today?" Where I had rehearsed for the last few years consciously and subconsciously the pain, the regret, the lie that "I am a terrible mother," now sitting before Jesus and Him saying, "Ask Me what I think of you as a mother" was the season shift, the new beginning. It was the heralding of the sun rising on a new day, like birds singing to welcome in the dawn.

This was the dawn. This was the dawn I had been waiting for.

His words would go forth from this place to transform and to open the way for a new day.

I could hear Song of Songs 2:11-13 (TPT):

> *The season has changed, the bondage of your barren winter has ended, and the season of hiding is over and gone. The rains have soaked the earth and left it bright with blossoming flowers. The season for singing and pruning the vines has arrived. I hear the cooing of doves in our land, filling the air with songs to awaken you and guide you forth. Can you not discern this new day of destiny breaking forth around you? The early signs of my purposes and plans are bursting forth. The budding vines of new life are now blooming everywhere. The fragrance of their flowers whispers, "There is change in the air."*

Now, the first step to stepping back into the place of governing in mothering for me looked like sitting at His feet, asking that question, and not stopping asking until He was done speaking. Day after day. Week after week. Month after month.

No longer rehearsing "I am a terrible mother," but rather rehearsing all HE said about who I was as a mother and how He saw me as a mother.

That's where I was called to sit and marinate, and that place would change everything.

So as we have journeyed through this chapter together, as I have invited you into part of my story as a mother, I want to encourage you. If you are reading this chapter and you have felt the pain, regret, and heartache I've walked, perhaps in a similar way or a very different way, whether you have children at home, your children are grown, you have spiritual children, grandchildren, or whatever your circumstance, my encouragement to you is to sit at His feet, sit at the feet of Jesus and ask Him, "What do You think of me as a mother?" And allow His Words of truth wash over you. Rehearse them and remain there.

That's the place where God will uproot things in the foundation that can hinder you from governing in mothering.

If you're flourishing in motherhood and in the place of your role as mother and you're feeling good right now, I rejoice with you and I am cheering you on, and I want to encourage you too. If you don't already, make it a regular space of communion with the Lord to ask Him to speak to you about how He sees you as a mother, and then find yourself undone again and again and again by His love.

In the next chapter, we look at "Ascended Mothering" and what it is to practically govern in mothering from the ascended place (Ephesians 2:6) and how that practically outworks in our homes and the lives of our children and families. But please do not be quick to move on to the next chapter.

Sit with Him and let Him love on you. This is probably a turning point for you.

Believe me, you're going to a whole new level of governing in mothering as a result of sitting at His feet.

# 11

# ASCENDED MOTHERING

As I wrote the last chapter on governing in mothering, I felt so strongly that there was most probably a turning point for you in the place of encounter, as you sat at His feet and you let Him love you and speak His words of truth over you in how He sees you as a mother. How one word out of His mouth changes everything, right?

I encourage you to not just sit in that place and allow the Lord to speak His truth over you about who you are as mother once, but sit there regularly, routinely. Parenting with the Holy Spirit is the best way to parent.

We are going to talk about greater practical ways to parent with the Holy Spirit in the next chapter, because as I sat with Jesus and leaned in to listen to His heart around "Ascended Mothering," I was overwhelmed by His heart of encouragement for you. I could feel the heart of the Lord say that before we proceed into some more practical ways of governing in mothering, the Lord had a word that He wanted to speak over you.

As we dive deep into this word together, I want to encourage you, before you read this word, I want you to quiet your heart and close your eyes and invite the Holy Spirit to come and to speak to you in this moment. That you would hear His voice and you would see the affection of the Lord's heart toward you. I see hope, healing, freedom, deliverance, strengthening, realignment, and fire being released right now to further empower and fill you afresh in your journey of mothering.

## Come Holy Spirit

I heard the Lord say, *"I am releasing recompense upon your rearing."*

Now, *rearing* is not a word I would usually use and honestly can't even remember a time when I have thought about that word or used it. So I looked up the definition of rearing. Rearing: To bring up and care for a child until they are fully grown. Synonyms: bring up, care for, look after, nurture, parent, educate, train, instruct, raise (Google).

Daughter of God, woman of God, *recompense is being released upon your rearing*. Nothing lost. Nothing wasted. In Him: *Restoration. Recompense. Renewal. Revival. Refreshment. Re-fueling.*

As I continued to seek the Lord I heard the Lord say:

> *Mothers, I am calling you to arise and take ground like never before in this hour. I have seen the battle that has been over your motherhood. The enemy has been pushing hard against your motherhood and many of you have found some of the greatest battles of your life have been fought in the area of mothering. For the enemy is after the next generation and the generations. The enemy is coming hard against My daughters and mothers in this hour, because this is the hour that I am raising up My Deborahs on earth to release the sound of the mother's roar to push back the kingdom of darkness and to see a mighty army of warriors arise in their children and the next generation and generations to usher in My glory.*
>
> *I have seen the tears, I have seen the heartache, I have seen the weariness, I have seen the confusion, the grief, the pain,*

*the discouragement, the attack that so many of you have endured. I have not stood idly on the sidelines and watched; I have been with you in the battle, strengthening you and calling you higher. I have been calling you into a new realm of governing in mothering; and I say unto you that in this season and this new era, you are coming into a new realm of governing in your mothering and learning in a greater way what it looks like to partner with Me in raising the children I have given you.*

*I am restoring to you the years that the locust has eaten and stolen, and in this season you shall see the recompense of My hand upon your rearing. You will see a greater manifestation of My power in your rearing. There is a* ***begin again*** *that I am declaring over your rearing, where you will see a supernatural expansion of time. I will bring forth fruitfulness in the areas the enemy has plundered and great shall be the health and wholeness in your land of rearing. I say unto you, no more barrenness over your rearing, but fruitfulness in your land of rearing. Supernatural strategies, insights and wisdom in your rearing where confusion, shame, and grief once took up residence. No more. Recompense and restoration upon your rearing.*

**Ascended mothering is found in a praying mother.**

I know in my own journey over the years of having four children that one of the biggest ways that the enemy can "get at me" is by attacking my children; one of the hardest places to navigate at times has been in the space of raising my children. Golly, the way the enemy's voice and my own voice can get *so* loud in my head around my parenting, as mentioned in the previous chapter, has been a *huge* battle. So in the place where I have sought the Lord about what it looks like to live in a place of ascended mothering, I knew it meant "living above," but how? As I leaned in and listened to the Lord, the words He spoke brought such a perspective shift in my life.

I heard the Lord say, *"Ascended mothering is found in a praying mother,"* and when the Lord spoke these words, I could feel the weight of His heart so strongly upon me.

To live as a woman of God fully alive in my mothering is one who mothers from the ascended place, and how do we do that? We pray and we pray at all times.

> *Rejoice always and delight in your faith;* ***be unceasing and persistent in prayer****; in every situation [no matter what the circumstances] be thankful and continually give thanks to God; for this is the will of God for you in Christ Jesus* (1 Thessalonians 5:16-18 AMP).

*"Be unceasing and persistent in prayer."* So as a mother, I want to be unceasing and persistent in prayer. As I have explored the invitation into *ascended mothering* from the Lord, I have realized how much I have lived "under" as a mother and how much I have taken on myself at times and not taken to prayer, not been unceasing and persistent in prayer.

But here's the thing, Mama, it's not from a place of striving. It's not from the place of anxiety and fear and having to constantly pray so that we are living and parenting from the ascended place and trying our best to "get there," it's recognizing that we do not parent alone. As a mama, I am raising my children with my incredible husband, but even more than that, I am parenting with the Holy Spirit.

I want you to truly grasp this, Mama. You are not alone and you do not parent alone, and living in the place of ascended mothering and governing mothering comes from a place of deep dependence and recognition upon Jesus and recognizing that you are not parenting alone.

You are parenting with Jesus. You are parenting with the Holy Spirit. I know when we have been mamas for a long time and walking with the Lord for a significant amount of time, we can "know" that truth, but then there are times and seasons when the pressure really comes on, chaos hits your home, attacks of the enemy comes against family and your children.

Then navigating the beautiful gift of raising children as they grow, you realize they have their own struggles, their own processes, their own challenges, that's when we really come to a place of knowing in a deeper way.

"I cannot do this without You, Lord."

Ever been there? I have...and the longer I am a mother, the more and more I am there, daily, multiple, multiple, multiple times a day.

So as we recognize our need for Him, we also recognize the beautiful truth of Psalm 46:1 (AMP):

> *God is our refuge and strength [mighty and impenetrable], a very present and well-proved help in trouble.*

My beautiful friend Katherine Ruonala says it this way, "He is my ever present help in time of need and my time of need is all the time."

And I will say, especially in mothering!

God is present and He is close and He is bringing us into a place of ascended mothering that lives from the seat of Ephesians 2:6, recognizing we are seated in heavenly places with Christ Jesus and we parent not alone.

So as we raise our children in this unstable and shaking earth right now, we are not raising weak, afraid "little humans," we are raising warriors, arrows, who are on earth to go glorify the Son Jesus Christ and extend His Kingdom. Mama, the enemy is terrified of them because as we raise our children knowing who Jesus is, discipling them in His ways and His Word, and testifying of the goodness of Almighty God and knowing who they are in Christ, we are raising children for such a time as this—they will be unstoppable in Christ, for His namesake.

I want you to think about this for a moment, the Lord said to me to *live in ascending mothering, as a praying mother.* This blows my mind. It's simple, deep, and profound.

As I raise my children from my knees in prayer, praying that I would be led and empowered to raise My children in His ways, reflecting Christ and His love and devoting them and my parenting to Him daily in prayer, recognizing I am parenting with the Holy Spirit—then *all strategies, wisdom, and solutions* are given to me as I seek Him. After all, He is the King of kings and Lord of lords, the One who created the heavens and the earth and all wisdom is found in Him (Colossians 2:3).

He has all the answers and He knows my children better than I do. He created them and He knows the exact ways for me to love my children the way they need to be loved, as He loves through me and knows exactly how I am to lead and guide them and raise them. What freedom! What rest is found in that place where the pressure comes off me to get everything right as a mother and I live as a surrendered, ascended, praying mother living deeply dependent upon the One who is my ever present help in time of need, to help me to raise my children in His ways.

Norwegian theologian and author Ole Hallesby said: "Pray for your children, night and day. Then you will leave them a great inheritance of answers to prayer, which will go with them as long as they live."

That quote completely undoes me. I sit here reading that quote again as I type it out, and as a mother my heart is gripped. All those moments when guilt, shame, and the enemy's voice has come against my mothering, right here in this quote is such instruction, such strategy, such hope, such revelation of living ascended as a mother. I am not only sowing into my children every day as I pray, I am leaving them an inheritance of answers to prayer, which will go with them as long as they live.

Wow!

Can you feel the call of the Lord's heart in this hour to arise as mama bears on earth to intercede, pray, and war over our children like never before? And the invitation into the heart of the Lord to receive His counsel and wisdom to pray His way, which will leave them with an inheritance of answered prayer.

Mama, hear me today and hear this. You are a powerful mama because you live *in Him* and He is the greatest parent ever. He is the perfect Father (Matthew 5:48) and *all* wisdom, strategy, and solution is given to you, *in Him!* Can you feel the rest, the hope and the strength in faith that the Lord is building within His mama bears in this hour? The roar that is being released in and from homes over a generation and generations that the enemy is trying to steal, kill, and destroy. Mama, you are one of the Lord's greatest weapons in this hour against the wiles and the plans of the evil one to destroy the generations and to destroy and kill our children. As you sit at His feet and as you pray, not only are you leaving them a great inheritance, you are posturing yourself to see the power of the Holy Spirit move through you in unprecedented ways to raise your children and lead them deeper into who He has created them to be—their true identity in Christ and their destiny.

No matter what has happened in the past, the pain that has remained in your mothering, this is a new day, and the Lord is heralding that over you today, Mama. Nothing is wasted, nothing is too far gone, the Lord is going to turn things around for you and your children *as you pray.*

And I prophesy over you today, though you may have endured years upon years of pain and heartache in your mothering journey and it has been such a battleground for you, the Lord says, *"As you pray, I can change things **in a day!**"*

Raise your faith, sweet mama, and arise, mama bear, because this is the end of a season of "living under," this is a new season of ascended mothering and God is calling us into the depths of His heart living as governing mothers, as we pray.

As a mother in this hour living surrendered, ascended, and praying, I must be a mother who *listens*. Listening prayer is so important for mothers. A governing mother mothers from the ascended place and listens to every word that the Lord speaks (Matthew 4:4). God speaks every day over our children, and we are to wait at wisdom's doorway daily to hear the word for every day (Proverbs 8:34-35 TPT) and align ourselves with the Word and the WAY (strategy) of God daily.

As we do this daily as mamas, the Spirit of God trains us to ascend above our emotions, our fears, our struggles and our mama guilt—and leads us into a place of peace, divine sight, and insight for our children as we raise them. Moment by moment, hour by hour, day by day.

As busy mamas, life can be very full, especially when our children are very young or we have multiple children. So how do we give God our full attention every day in the midst of nappies (changing diapers), playing with our children and their toys, feeding them, doing school drop-offs, laundry, etc. (Oh don't get me started about how my laundry pile has the gift of constant multiplication.) I believe we can accomplish it all by practicing the presence of God.

Ascended mothering and governing mothering happens as we learn to train ourselves to practice the presence of God, as we ABIDE in Him (John 15).

John Mark Comer, in his book *Practicing the Way*, talks about "Turning God Into a Habit," and he references Brother Lawrence, whose story has had a tremendous impact on my life. In his book Comer writes:

> The monk who coined the phrase "The practice of the presence of God" wasn't a priest; he was a dishwasher in a monastery in seventeenth century Paris. Brother Lawrence made it his life's ambition to experience God in the chaos of the kitchen, with all its noise, distraction, and busyness. By the end of his life he said, "the time of busyness does not with me differ from the time of prayer; and in the noise and clatter of my kitchen, while several persons are at the same time calling for different things, I possess God in as great tranquility as if I were upon my knees before the Blessed Sacrament."

John Mark goes on to say:

> Take note: He was Catholic. The "Blessed Sacrament" (what Protestants call "the Lord's supper") was the holiest moment in the spiritual life. But Brother Lawrence had come to a place where ALL of his life was holy; there was no longer any difference between the quiet of morning prayer and the cacophony of dinner prep, between the sanctity of the altar and the mundanity of the evening meal. Life was a seamless, integrated, whole, grounded in God's presence. (p. 41-42)

Coming back to what the Lord said to me, *"Ascended Mothering is found in a praying mother,"* and reflecting on 1 Thessalonians 5: 16-18 being unceasing and persistent in prayer, how can we do that?

We can *turn God into a habit* like Brother Lawrence, practicing the presence of God in the midst of mama life. We can train ourselves to be in a space of constantly communing with the Lord every day as we raise our children.

It is about turning our affection and attention toward Him throughout the day as we raise our children. It's training ourselves to not only have those special moments tucked away with Him when we can pray over and for our children, it's the moments when we are cooking dinner and we pray for our children, we invite the Holy Spirit continually throughout our day to come and speak. We need to learn to listen as we wash dishes, to pause in the moments of chaos and tantrums or teenagers having a meltdown in our lounge room, to pause, to breathe, and to lift our eyes to where our help comes from (Psalm 121) and ask Him for help, strategy, and divine insight.

We are coming up higher, Mama. The strategy, wisdom, and divine insight the Lord is releasing to us mamas in this hour to pray, train, lead, and nurture our children for this day that we live in and that they will live in, will arm and strengthen them for the days ahead and for all the Lord calls them to do.

Arise, Mama Bears! The Lord is increasing the roar within you of militant intercession for your children and for the generations.

Remember the Lord's words, *"Ascended mothering is found in a prayer mother."*

The *mama bear roar* is being released on earth in militant intercession and bold declaration of truth that will see these ones given into our care shot out into the world like arrows as friends of Jesus. They will release His love and proclaim the Good News of the gospel, piercing the darkness with the light and glory of Jesus, extending His Kingdom in bold and unapologetic ways. Watch the level of faith these ones will walk in, the mighty exploits they will do in His name, and His power will be displayed through them as these bold generations arise.

# 12

# "CAN YOU HEAR...THE THUNDER IN THEIR STEPS?"

Recently, I heard the Lord say, "*Can you hear the sound of the army of My daughters who are arising in this hour with thunder in their steps?*"

As I heard the Lord speak those words, do you know what I heard? I heard the sound of an army of women, marching arm in arm, shoulder to shoulder, *fully alive*. The atmosphere was so full of authority and strength. The thundering of the steps I heard would cause mountains to crumble. There was a strength within them that came from not their own efforts but from the deep place of intimacy with Jesus. It came from the place of knowing Him deeply and then walking as those who walk as one—those who know Him and walk His way.

The atmosphere was full of boldness as this army of His daughters arose. Their boldness came from knowing who He is, and I heard the Lord say, "*Look closely, Lana,*" and I leaned in and looked closer. As I did, I heard the Lord say, "*There is no fear. See there is no fear, they have been with Me.*"

In that moment I could feel Acts 4:13 (AMP) surrounding me:

> *Now when the men of the Sanhedrin (Jewish High Court) saw the confidence and boldness off Peter and John, and grasped*

> *the fact that they were uneducated and untrained [ordinary] men, they were astounded, and began to recognize that they had been with Jesus.*

The council members were astonished as they witnessed the bold courage of Peter and John, especially when they discovered that they were just ordinary men who had never had religious training. Then they began to understand the effect Jesus had on them by spending time with Him.

Here we have the men of the Sanhedrin astounded and astonished by the confidence and boldness of Peter and John. Why? Because they had been with Jesus. Because of the effect Jesus had on them by spending time with Him.

They began to recognize that they had been with Jesus!

The atmosphere that surrounded me in this encounter was one of such boldness that as the Lord caused this army of daughters to arise, they were arising *unashamed and unafraid!*

As the Lord spoke, I was reminded of Joan of Arc and her assignment to lead France to victory as she led the French army in its war with England and where she spoke to her soldiers:

> It's not enough that God be with us. We must be with God.... I would rather die than do something which I know to be a sin, or be against God's will. Act and God will Act.

Talk about boldness! Joan of Arc's ferocious boldness and conviction is coming on His daughters afresh, obeying the Lord even unto death. Joan of Arc was captured by the enemy forces, tried for witchcraft, and burned at the stake at the age of 19. By the time she was canonized in 1920, Joan of Arc was considered one of history's greatest martyrs and the patron saint of France.[3]

"It's not enough that God be with us, we must be with God"—that ferocious fire and boldness is upon today's army of daughters of God who give the Lord their *yes* in this hour to do mighty things with Him.

The religious boxes of the "shoulds" and human expectations are being broken off His daughters, and they are arising in this hour, fully alive and deeply rooted. As I looked at this army of women arising I heard myself say, "They cannot be moved or shaken because they have been *overtaken* by the Lord God."

The Lord then spoke:

> *Here they come, here they come. My daughters arising with thunder in their steps because they walk in Me and they carry My prophetic voice and they carry My heart. They are consumed with My Word, they are consumed with My fire, they are consumed with My heart. Can you hear the sound of an army arising with thunder in their steps? Here they come, arising out of the wilderness, leaning upon their Beloved. They are not the ones who parade revelation. They are pure. Their hearts before Me are pure as they live before the audience of One. They are the unapologetic ones. They are the ones who have been through My unrelenting fire and have been* ***consumed.*** *They arise* ***consumed.*** *They are arising* ***consumed*** *with My fire and* ***no longer*** *contained.*
>
> *They are arising in obedience, far from defeat, as they have lived deeply at My feet. Here they come arising on earth to take authority and dominion for My Kingdom. No longer will they be harassed by the enemy, no longer will they live assaulted by the Jezebellic spirit. For in the secret place they have been trained for war. I have trained their fingers for*

*war and their hands for battle (Psalm 144:1). They live so deeply connected to Me for their greatest desire is to abide. The enemy has screamed at them to* ***pause and retreat,*** *and I am speaking over them to* ***push and defeat.*** *It is time for them to arise in their destiny in greater ways, awakened to My authority within them; they arise not in arrogance but in confidence of who I am in them and who they are in Me.*

As His voice surrounded me, freedom resounded, thundering in complete and total heavenly unison with Esther 4:14 (AMP):

> *For if you remain silent at this time, liberation and rescue will arise for the Jews from another place, and you and your father's house will perish [since you did not help when you had the chance]. And who knows whether you have attained royalty for such a time as this [and for this very purpose]?*

The urgency of the hour surrounded me. The urgency of the hour for His daughters to arise with a bold YES to Him that springs forth from their laid-down place of devotion and adoration of Him. There was a divine convergence happening in this season where preparation of many previous seasons were colliding into this new era and positioning His daughters to arise in their destiny in ways that they had not seen before. The urgency of the hour in which we live demanded an *"all in yes"* to Jesus.

The words in brackets in the Amplified version, *"since you did not help when you had the chance,"* struck me deeply. As I read those words, not only was I surrounded by the Spirit of God so loudly highlighting this verse for this hour and the urgency of it, it took me back to an encounter I had at the start of 2024.

In the night hours I heard the Lord's voice so strongly, so loudly with such intense authority. He said:

*The Church needs to stop acting like a doll on a stand and be the city on the hill that I have created her to be.*

When He spoke those words, I felt the fear of the Lord upon them and the heralding of the Lord's heart that right now is time for His Church to *engage* and to *be* the city on the hill (Matthew 5:14). Not like a doll on a stand that is to be admired while sitting on a shelf, gathering dust and looking beautiful but *doing nothing.* God is calling the Church to *be* the city on the hill that cannot be hidden, to be the beacon of light in the night, releasing His light to a very broken, lost, and dying world. To be a city on a hill helping people to see, bringing direction, bringing hope, being a guiding light from a *higher position.*

As we live before His face, as we live beholding His beauty, living in the light of His face, eye to eye, seeing as He sees, in that place of deep intimacy, we reflect His light, His truth, His glory, His Word into the world to draw others to Him, to bring hope, shift atmospheres, and see His Kingdom come on earth, through you and me.

The Lord is calling us to engage, to arise and take our place, whatever that looks like for us individually as daughters of God. As each one of us arise and take our place, then together collectively we arise as an unstoppable army moving forward with thunder in our steps as HIS presence and Word goes out from our lives to accomplish HIS purposes and plans on earth and make way for His glory. It's time to come out! I hear the Lord calling His daughters, "*Come out of hiding.*"

The hour is urgent, the call is loud, arise with your Beloved and take your place. Be in the secret place with the Lord and allow the fire of God to consume you. Ask the Holy Spirit to do the heart surgery if needed, if there are things hindering your "Yes" to Him, your "All in yes" to Him; because daughter, listen to me, the world needs you. The world needs your history and relationship with God to shine brightly on earth and for you to be who you were created to be.

The world needs to see the Jesus *in you!* You have a part to play in this hour. What is it? Have you asked Him? Let us not be found wanting when the Lord calls to us in this hour. Let us not be found wanting in the place of *"you did not help when you had the chance"* (Esther 4:14).

This is not a place for condemnation, this is a place of recognizing the urgency of the hour in which we live; and you are being called for such a time as this. He is calling you to arise, daughter, receive a fresh baptism of His fire, and embrace the fire that ignites a "No toleration" roar within you that says, "I won't allow *anything* to stop me *anymore* from being who God has created me to be and doing what God has created me to do. Fire of God consume me!"

From that place, you arise and continue to arise, daughter of Zion, warrior of God, unstoppable, not from your own strength but recognizing who you live *in* and whose you *are*. Who goes with you in the urgency of the hour! The Lord began to show me how so many daughters had been battling with strongholds of fear. Some of them for their whole lives, others in seasons, and now is the season of complete freedom. Now is the season of His daughters arising in boldness and power, His power, from a place of deep tenderness toward His heart and living deeply in the fear of the Lord. They are arising and the Spirit of God is shifting them *suddenly* from *fearful to fierce*. From *weary to fortified, empowered, and strengthened.*

His voice surrounded me again:

> *My daughter, could it be possible that I am raising up a company of women in this hour who are fearless and fear is no longer part of the equation or conversation? As I raise up an army of daughters who know that all they need is Me and* ***nothing is impossible.***

> *These daughters, they live* **in and before** *My face and they do not move. They are ferociously focused upon My face and feasting upon My Word, and they do not move. Watch how they will arise in this hour with the ferocious focus of faith. They will take Me at My Word, and they will be unapologetic of My Word in their mouth and the fire in their bellies.*

Then His voice thundered around me:

> ***No longer will they cower, they will move in My power.***

Daughter of God, I want to pause here for a moment. You may be reading this encounter and reading the words flowing from the heart of God and saying, "But Lana, I don't feel like I am anywhere near this. In fact, I feel deeply fearful. I still haven't received my healing, my breakthrough, and I certainly don't feel fully alive. I still feel broken, weary, heavy-hearted, this doesn't feel like me at all."

If that's you, I feel the Spirit of God wanting me to encourage you right now. Let's first take the word *feel* out of the conversation. Sure, we all "feel" certain ways and feelings are strong, they are loud, and feelings are not to be condemned or ignored, *but* they are not to be what leads us. They are not to be our loudest voice.

The consuming fire of the Lord is heavily upon His daughters in this hour and upon the Church. God is consuming all that is not of Him within us, and He is igniting all things that are of Him. Part of the move of His fire that is consuming, I believe, is bringing a realignment in our hearts, from being led or governed by emotions, to led and governed by the Spirit of God, faith. It doesn't deny pain, hurt, grief, and things that we experience in life, but it doesn't give it the loudest voice.

If we as His daughters arise in this hour led by what we "feel," we will be far from fortified. The Lord is calling us higher. He is calling us to live by faith in a greater way than we ever have before. Stretching? Absolutely! Necessary? *Absolutely!*

So as we journey together through what the Lord is speaking in this chapter, I want to challenge you—if those "I feel" words and emotions are screaming loudly at you, take your eyes off what you feel and place them on what He is speaking here, by faith. The Lord wants to ignite hope, ignite faith, and ignite strength within you that this is what He is doing. You are being called as part of this army. He is beckoning you. Wooing you. Encouraging you, "Daughter, I am *restoring all.*"

I hear the Lord saying, *"It will be as if it never was."*

The level of restoration and divine positioning and the shift and move of His Spirit in your life that *will* and *is* taking place as you give Him your *yes* afresh causes you to move forth in obedience to Him and His ways. You are aligning with the trumpet sound, the clarion call that is being released on earth right now to "Arise and take your place." As all this happens, you will see a powerful demonstration of His power in your life to restore you, strengthen you, reposition you, and see you arise *out* of your wilderness leaning on your Beloved (Song of Songs 8:5).

You will walk in a new level of divine restoration, healing, and recompense as if you never experienced what the evil one meant for your destruction. Rather, the restoring, powerful hand of the Lord has moved powerfully upon you, in you, and in your life to completely refresh you wholly.

So as we now continue in what the Lord is speaking, grab this by faith—it's a new day for you, precious daughter of God.

# 13

# GOD IS ARMING HIS DAUGHTERS WITH STRENGTH AND STRATEGY

I hear the Lord saying, "*Here come My warrior women of wisdom arising in greater ways in this hour.*"

Daughter of God, precious woman of God, there is an invitation that I am feeling weightier than I have ever felt it into the wisdom of God in this hour. James 1:5 (ESV) says:

> *If any of you lacks wisdom, let him ask God, who gives generously to all without reproach, and it will be given him.*

Proverbs 4:7 (TPT) says:

> *Wisdom is the most valuable commodity—so buy it! Revelation-knowledge is what you need—so invest in it.*

> *A warrior filled with wisdom ascends into the high place and releases breakthrough, bringing down the strongholds of the mighty* (Proverbs 21:22 TPT).

Brian Simmons in his commentary notes on this verse says, "demolishing their strength of confidence."

This is the hour when we must cry out for wisdom and understanding like never before, the hour requires it; God is raising up His warrior women of wisdom in this hour in powerful and never-seen-before ways.

I know for many incredible daughters, the seasons have been full of intense battles and many trials, but the prophetic voice of God is thundering over you:

> *Arise, warrior women of wisdom! Receive My supernatural refreshment and strength in this hour. My precious daughter, I am releasing rapid refreshment upon you in this hour, where I am not only washing away weariness, but I am* ***infusing*** *you with My strength to restore you in every way. I am bringing forth that rapid refreshment and a rapid restoration of* ***resolve.*** *The enemy has come hard after you with weariness because he is after your resolve. He is after your faith! For I say to you that in this hour I am raising up an army of bold, passionate women as ones who are ferociously focused upon Me and living by faith not by sight on a level and in a depth you have not walked in before.*

Receive His words over you today: "*I am arming you with strength and strategy for the days ahead.*"

I hear the whisper of His heart over you:

> *My precious daughters, align not with weariness, align not with weakness, align not with the narrative of the enemy of survival mode. I am raising you up within My army as strong warriors, strong not in your own strength, but strong*

*in the place of reliance, resilience, and dependence upon Me—completely infused and saturated in the empowerment and strength of My Spirit. The rapid refreshment that I am releasing in this hour will not just restore you, it will increase you like you have not yet known. You will be left in awe and wonder of My power in your life as you see this refreshment not only restore you and your resolve, but position you to govern with Me in these days like never before.*

*In the rapid refreshment and rapid restoration of resolve that I am bringing forth in your life, you will see great victory. Pay attention to the areas where there has been the greatest weariness and attack on your strength and resolve, and watch what I will do and am doing, My daughters, as the power of My Spirit moves through you in ways you've never seen to bring forth unprecedented demonstrations of My victory and power.*

Daughter of God, the Lord is washing away weariness in your life, and there is an invitation before you to live and walk in His heavenly wisdom on a level you have not walked in before.

The enemy has worked so hard to strip you of the revelation of your authority and identity in Christ, but God has been and is restoring these revelations in your heart and life. You are a precious, loved, beautiful, cherished, forgiven, righteous daughter of God. There is an accelerated great awakening that has been blowing fiercely upon you to cause you to arise and stand like never before.

In this era when the Lord is releasing supernatural strategy, divine intel, and wisdom on an unprecedented scale, He is infusing you with strength to restore you in every way. Weariness attempted to weaken your resolve, and the enemy has come hard after you with weariness because he is after your resolve, he has been after your faith. Woman of God, the Lord is raising you up in this hour from a deep place of weariness to a place of rest and dependence on Him in the place of intimacy where the waterfall of His love cascades over you and supernaturally infuses you with His strength again.

I heard the Lord say,

> *There has been a war over discernment, where weariness has tried to confuse you and weaken your discernment. Oh watch the power of My hand not only break off this weariness through the rapid refreshment I am releasing, but I will increase your insight and discernment to see and uncover the plans of the enemy and discern My plans and purposes in the days ahead to know My ways in greater ways and move forth with Me to establish what I am bringing forth on earth.*
>
> *The enemy has done all he can to attempt to weary you so you will come off the wall of watching to build My Kingdom. But I say unto you, as you have continued to remain, I am now supernaturally increasing your capacity, your strength, and your resolve to move with Me into new assignments with a renewed strength. My wind is blowing and My wind is blowing fiercely. As you continue to rise on the wings of My wind—the wind of My Spirit—you are being brought into a supernatural strength you have not experienced before.*

Daughter of God, I feel His heart for you deeply. If you find yourself weary, I encourage you to not align with weariness, do not alight with the narrative of the enemy of survival mode. God is raising you up as part of an army of strong, resilient, bold warrior women in this hour who are completely infused and saturated in the empowerment and strength of His Spirit.

## Turn Your Mind Toward God

There is a mighty turning taking place, and I hear the Lord say, ***"Now turn your mind toward Me."***

There has been such a battle of the mind and warfare of the mind that has increased significantly in this season. And as the call of the Lord has been extended to His Bride to ascend and come up higher, the prophetic standard the Lord has set in this hour to ascend has been revealed. There has also been a great revealing of the warfare against the mind and the unrenewed mind.

There is a very clear link between the renewing of the mind and discernment that is found in Romans 12:1-2 (NKJV):

> *I beseech you therefore, brethren, by the mercies of God, that you present your bodies a living sacrifice, holy, acceptable to God, which is your reasonable service.* ***And do not be conformed to this world, but be transformed by the renewing of your mind, that you may prove what is that good and acceptable and perfect will of God.***

The Lord is calling us as His daughters to turn our minds toward Him. I hear the Lord saying, "*Worship Me with your thoughts, worship Me with your mind, worship Me with your expectations.*"

Doesn't that shift your perspective? Every thought I have should prompt me to ask myself, "Is this a thought that worships and exalts Jesus? Or is it in opposition to the knowledge of God?" God is calling us to get even more violent in our renewal of the mind. So I am going to choose to worship God with my thoughts, with my mind and my expectations by taking every thought captive that is not in line with who He is and His nature and truth and worship Him by replacing it with His Word.

Second Corinthians 10:5 (NIV) says, ***"We demolish arguments and every pretension that sets itself up against the knowledge of***

*God, and we take captive every thought to make it obedient to Christ."*

I love in Psalm 119:169 (NLT) where David says, "*O Lord, listen to my cry; give me the discerning mind you promised.*"

And here we are now, living in Christ; in Him we live and move and have our being (Acts 17:28), and we have the mind of Christ (1 Corinthians 2:16). Wow! Woman of God, daughter of God, think about this for a second, in Christ you have the gift of supernatural empowerment and grace to renew your mind and walk in the mind of Christ.

In this hour, God is raising up women in greater ways who live not as victims to mindsets and assaults from the enemy upon their minds leaving them condemned, feeling defeated, and like they are constantly living "under" their thoughts anymore. There is a great awakening taking place in the lives of His daughters in this hour, an increased fire of intolerance against the onslaught of the enemy against their minds and in a greater way and with greater empowerment and grace. They have the power to fiercely go after every thought and take it captive and to live fully alive by being daughters of God who walk constantly growing up into and awakened to the revelation that they have the mind of Christ.

It doesn't mean that the battle of the mind is suddenly ending, but it does mean that the Lord is awakening His daughters to biblical truths and the power of the Word and the weapon of the Word in their hands to *overcome* in their minds in a way they have not experienced before. That's for you, daughter of God. The Lord is causing you to awaken in a greater way and understand what it looks like to live as a woman of God *fully alive* with a renewed mind.

**We are living in an era of unprecedented acceleration of supernatural strategy, insight, divine intel, and wisdom.**

I believe the Lord has been calling us up higher to ascend in how we think and the importance of seeing from His perspective and walking by faith, not by sight. As I have leaned in and listened to what is on the Lord's heart, He has been speaking to me about this current era; it is one of unprecedented acceleration of supernatural strategy, divine insight and sight, divine intel and wisdom.

I believe we have been called into the secret place to *hear, receive, and perceive what the Spirit of the Lord is saying and His strategy, wisdom and intel from Him in a greater way than we have ever received, to partner with Him in intercession and building in this hour.*

Like in Nehemiah 4:17 (AMP), "*Those who were rebuilding the wall and those who carried burdens loaded themselves so that everyone worked with one hand and held a weapon with the other.*"

The Benson Commentary on Biblehub.com says of Nehemiah 4:17: "That is, they were well prepared either to build or fight; for the expression is figurative. It is not possible for them to work, if both hands had not been at liberty. Accordingly the next verse says, '*Everyone had his sword girded by his side.*' Thus we must work out our salvation, with the weapons of warfare in our hands. For in every duty we must expect opposition from our spiritual enemies."

The Matthew Henry Commentary says of Nehemiah 4:16-23: "We must watch against spiritual enemies, and not expect that our warfare will be over till our work is ended. The Word of God is the sword of the Spirit, which we ought to have always at hand, and never to have to seek for it, either in our labors, or in our conflicts as Christians. Every true Christian is both a laborer and a soldier, working with one hand, and fighting with the other."

God is arming His daughters in this hour with strength and strategy. He has been working deeply within you as you have embraced the refiners fire strengthening you as a laborer/builder and a soldier/warrior. There has been much resistance training, but in this season as you stay nestled in the secret place communing with Him and listening to His voice, there is a greater empowerment and grace being released into your life to build and fight from the place of deep intimacy with Him and to receive His intel and His wisdom. In this season we need to not only know the *way* of God, we need to know the *mind* of the Lord too. How He thinks and align ourselves with that.

The depth of the invitation being extended to us as His daughters in this hour to live deeply in the Word, *know* the Word, and *walk in* the Word is urgent. With the rise of deception, false teaching, and worldly narratives that have entered the Church, we have to be people who *love* the Word of God and hold the Word of God as the ultimate truth and inspired Word of the Lord.

As His daughters, the Lord is calling us deeper into the Bible. He is increasing hunger for the Word. I believe there is a Bible revival on the heart of the Lord to bring His people back to and deeper into solid, biblical truths and foundations. *There* we find strength in Him, His words—the infallible Word of God. Any deviation from the Word is deception.

God is raising up women who live fully alive as they feast on, obey, and walk in the Word of God that is alive and active and sharper than a two-edged sword (Hebrews 4:12).

I remember an encounter I had when I was living in South Australia a number of years ago and I woke up in the middle of the night to go to the bathroom. As I rolled over and my feet hit the floor and I got up to walk, I took a few steps and was unable to move as the weight of the Lord's presence filled my room so significantly. I then heard the Lord say, "*Lana, I want to show you something.*"

## A Vision, an Invitation

Before my eyes a vision opened up, and I began to see a scroll coming out of Heaven and unraveling before my eyes. Upon this scroll I watched as things began to download, and as I watched in my spirit, I knew that this scroll represented blueprints and strategies for this season.

The Lord then spoke, "*In the new era I will release* ***intricate instruction****, strategies, and blueprints to know My ways to build with Me.*"

I was struck in that moment that there was coming an invitation into accessing and living in a realm of divine wisdom as God's people that we had not yet experienced. I felt the fear of the Lord all over me as I could feel the weight of what we were being invited into and a strong sense of it's not just something that we will receive as we sit on our hands and wait for it. It is an invitation from the Lord that requires a response, it requires our yes and our alignment.

I believe we have arrived in this season now where the Lord is calling us into His wisdom, to know His wisdom and walk in it, in ways we have not yet known.

As I have sought the Lord, the Lord took me to Proverbs 2:1-7:

> *My son* ***if*** *you will receive My words and treasure my commandments within you, so that your ear is attentive to [skillful and godly] wisdom, and apply your heart to understanding [seeking it conscientiously and striving for it eagerly]; yes, if you cry out for insight, and lift up your voice for understanding;* ***if*** *you will seek skillful and godly wisdom as you would silver and search for her as you would hidden treasures; then you will understand the [reverent] fear of the Lord, [that is worshiping Him and regarding*

*Him as truly awesome] and discover the knowledge of God. For the Lord gives [skillful and godly] wisdom; from His mouth comes knowledge and understanding. He stores away sound wisdom for the righteous, [those who are in right standing with Him]; He is a shield to those who walk in integrity [those of honorable character and moral courage]* (AMP).

*My child, will you treasure my wisdom? Then, and only then, will you acquire it. And only if you accept my advice and hide it within you will you succeed. So train your heart to listen when I speak and open your spirit wide to expand your discernment—then pass it on to your sons and daughters. Yes, cry out for comprehension and intercede for insight. For if you keep seeking it like a man would seek for sterling silver, searching in hidden places for cherished treasure, then you will discover the fear of the Lord and find the true knowledge of God. Wisdom is a gift from a generous God, and every word He speaks is full of revelation and becomes a foundation of understanding within you. For the Lord has a hidden storehouse of wisdom made accessible to his godly ones. He becomes your personal bodyguard as you follow his ways, protecting and guarding you as you choose what is right. Then you will discover all that is just, proper, fair and be empowered to make the right decisions as you walk into your destiny* (Proverbs 2:1-9 TPT).

As the Lord is increasing divine intel in this hour and inviting us deeper into receiving and walking in His wisdom, there are keys contained within this Scripture passage that we need to adhere to.

I want you to look at both of those translations and notice the word *if* mentioned in both:

> *My son if you will receive My words and treasure my commandments within you...* (AMP).
>
> *My child, will you treasure My wisdom? Then, and only then, will you acquire it. And only if you accept My advice, hide it within you, will you succeed* (TPT).

As the Lord is calling us deeper into the place of receiving divine intel from His heart and wisdom in this hour, we will only receive His wisdom if we *receive* and treasure His commandments within us; and if we treasure His wisdom and accept His advice, *then* we will acquire it.

Can you feel the fear of the Lord on those Scripture verses? The call in this hour to receive, perceive, and walk in the wisdom of God cannot be entered into *if:*

1. We are not walking in the fear of the Lord.
2. We do not treasure His wisdom, His words, and His commandments *above all else.*

His ways, His Word, His commandments have the highest place in my life, because of *whose* Word it is. If the heart is complacent or becomes familiar and there's a lack of treasuring the wisdom and commands of the Lord, we will not acquire it.

Let's look at verses 2-4 in Proverbs 2:

> *So that your ear is attentive to [skillful and godly] wisdom, and apply your heart to understanding [seeking it conscientiously and striving for it eagerly]; yes, if you cry out for insight, and lift up your voice for understanding; if you will seek skillful and godly wisdom as you would silver and search for her as you would hidden treasures* (AMP).

> *So train your heart to listen when I speak and open your spirit wide to expand your discernment—then pass it on to your sons and daughters. Yes, cry out for comprehension and intercede for insight. For is you keep seeking it like a man would seek for sterling silver, searching in hidden places for cherished treasure* (TPT).

Oh the glorious keys the Holy Spirit reveals through this passage for us to posture ourselves in this season.

As God is inviting us into a deeper space of receiving, hearing, and perceiving His divine intel and wisdom, we must:

- Have ears that are attentive to His wisdom.
- Apply our hearts to understanding. (I love this! Seeking it *conscientiously* and *striving for it eagerly!) So your ear is* attentive to wisdom and apply your heart to understanding.
- Cry out for insight.
- Lift up our voice for understanding.

Let's look at these words for a moment. None of these words speak "sit on the sideline and wait for wisdom." No. These words *shout* desperation for His wisdom and a desperate *need* for the wisdom of God in our lives and chasing hard after it, eagerly, conscientiously, striving for it, interceding for insight like it says in The Passion Translation, *searching for it in hidden places, training our hearts to listen, opening our spirits wide to expand our discernment....*

This is a violent, ferocious posture of desperation, I *must* have Your wisdom, Lord.

Woman of God, daughter of God, can you feel the Spirit moving amidst this? He is awakening us as His daughters and the Bride of Christ as a whole in this hour to our need for His wisdom and our lack of understanding and earthly wisdom. It's not a place of condemnation, it's a place of awe and wonder recognizing *who He is*—He is God Almighty and His wisdom is so far above our mere human wisdom.

Daughter, we are being invited in a greater way in this hour *into* living more deeply in His wisdom as we treasure His Word and commandments, His wisdom, *above all;* oh the mysteries and strategies He is inviting us into in a deeper way to see *His* Kingdom extended on earth.

> *For who can know the Lord's thoughts? Who knows enough to give him advice? And who has given him so much that he needs to pay it back? For everything comes from him and exists by his power and is intended for his glory. All glory to him forever! Amen* (Romans 11:34-36 NLT).

Proverbs 9:10 (NKJV) says, "*The fear of the Lord is the beginning of wisdom, and the knowledge of the Holy One is understanding,*" and couple this Scripture with Proverbs 2:5 (AMP), "*Then you will understand the [reverent] fear of the Lord, [that is worshiping Him and regarding Him as truly awesome] and discover the knowledge of God.*"

This is very important, daughter of God, let's look at this more closely.

I believe that the fear of the Lord bookends wisdom. Let me explain. Proverbs 2 says that the fear of the Lord is the *beginning* of wisdom. Why?

Because I recognize *my need* for His wisdom, if I approach the Lord and ask for wisdom (James 1:5), I recognize how finite my wisdom is and how in need of His wisdom I am. I recognize *whose* wisdom it is and how almighty He is and perfect are His ways (Psalm 18:30). I come in humility and reverence for who He is and I ask to receive. As I come in the fear of the Lord and I approach in humility,

I receive His wisdom; then *as* I receive His wisdom, I am left in awe and wonder again of who He is, and I walk deeper and deeper in the fear of the Lord.

In this hour there is a mighty dealing of the Lord's hand against pride and against exalted opinion. *Why?* Because He wants to raise up His beautiful Bride, pure and without spot or wrinkle, walking in the fear of the Lord and *His* wisdom. He wants to see His power demonstrated through His beautiful Bride in the nations, in a stunning, beautiful, and thunderous way.

Psalm 25:14 (NIV) says, *"The Lord confides in those who fear him; he makes his covenant known to them."*

The King James Version says it this way: *"The secret of the Lord is with them that fear him."* Strong's Concordance cites the Hebrew word for *secret* in Psalm 25:14 is *sod,* which means "counsel, intimacy, a session (company of persons in close deliberation)."

Wow! The Lord *confides* His secrets and His counsel with those who live in deep intimacy with Him. I have had numerous encounters in this season where I see the eyes of the Lord roaming the earth looking for those whose hearts are fully His and will steward the secrets of His heart with purity, integrity, humility, and secrecy (when He tells you to be quiet).

In order to carry His wisdom in this hour, I believe we have to lay down our own understanding. We have to lay down our right to understand. We have to lay down our own opinions, presumptions, and assumptions. I remember when I wrote my book, *I Hear the Lord Say New Era,*[4] the Lord said to me that one of the greatest traps His people could get caught in, in the new era, was to live in the place of assumption or presumption. We "assume or presume" how He is going to move, what it's going to look like, how the outcome will manifest, when it will manifest, etc. (Have you been there? And it's so easy to do! Or is that just me at times?!) But God is calling us into a deeper place of surrender and abandonment to His ways and His wisdom.

If His wisdom says, "Build a boat" and you don't even know what rain is and people think you're crazy, you build that boat because it's His wisdom. It's His strategy—and in order to walk in His wisdom and strategy in this hour when we see His glory manifested and revelation of His majesty on earth like never seen before, we must be living in the fear of the Lord and in humility. The door to ascend, to come up higher in wisdom, is found on the floor, the place of surrender. The door is in the floor. Lower and lower still.

Proverbs 3:5-6 (AMP) is a key Scripture in this hour as God releases His wisdom to those who will seek Him earnestly:

> *Trust in and rely confidently on the Lord with all your heart and do not rely on your own insight or understanding. In all your ways know and acknowledge and recognize Him, and He will make your paths straight and smooth [removing obstacles that block your way].*

He is raising up powerful women of wisdom, who are carrying not their own wisdom, but the fountain of wisdom, Christ flowing through their lives guiding them, directing them, leading them—and releasing wisdom and insight through them to others and to nations.

I want you to pause and reflect on the invitation being extended by the Lord to us in this hour. Let us posture ourselves and our hearts before Him to love Him, minister to Him, know Him deeply, and know His heart and mind in this hour.

There is a powerful move of God among women where He is raising them up living fully alive, fully aware, and fully awake in ways we have NEVER seen before. They have the mind of Christ (1 Corinthians 2:16) to walk in it and to conscientiously seek His mind, His thoughts, His strategies, His wisdom, His intel, to build and see the Kingdom established and the glory of the Lord manifested on earth.

As we wrap up this chapter, let's look at 1 Corinthians 2:16 in context of all the Lord has spoken in this chapter from the Amplified Classic Bible:

> *For who has known or understood the mind (the counsels and purposes) of the Lord so as to guide and instruct Him and give Him knowledge? But we have the mind of Christ (the Messiah) and do hold the thoughts (feelings and purposes) of His heart.*

We have moved into a greater awakening of our governmental authority and reigning and co-laboring with Him in this season, which will continue to increase and increase to see His Kingdom come.

Woman of wisdom, it's your time to *arise* and be *wowed* by His wisdom and see the earth *marvel* at His ways.

14

# GOD IS RAISING DAUGHTERS OF DISCERNMENT

Daughter of God, as we dive into this chapter together, before we really even get deeply into it, there's something I need to say to you. There's something that has gripped my heart deeply from the Father's heart for you and I want you to hear this and I want to encourage you to not quickly pass it by but allow this phrase to sit strongly in your heart and your spirit: ***"Do not doubt your discernment now or in the days ahead."***

The Lord showed me that many have dismissed their discernment, tried to rationalize their discernment, or dumb it down. The Lord is actually bringing forth in this hour a company of women, His daughters worldwide living fully alive, walking in discernment, and ever growing in the journey of being discipled by the Lord.

Let's stop there for a second and look at the words: *"ever growing in the journey of being discipled by the Lord."*

As we dive into this chapter, I want to say this. If we ever think we have "arrived," have discernment down pat, have the best discernment around, and are not teachable—we have entered into very dangerous ground. We are *ever* growing in maturing into discernment as the Lord disciples us in it and having trusted community and accountability around us to weigh discernment.

The very heart of this chapter is the Lord raising up daughters of discernment from a place of humility, of teachability, of being deeply surrendered to the Lord and recognizing they are ever, always growing.

I was deeply gripped by the heart of the Lord for the daughters who have been discerning rightly from the Lord things that He has been sharing with them, yet they have been so tormented, clouded, and chained in doubt. If that's you, the Lord wants to minister to you in this chapter, while also releasing some prophetic insight for the days ahead.

Let's continue.

The words, *"Do not doubt your discernment in the days ahead,"* are not words unfamiliar to me. These are words I have wrestled with at many points in my life, especially in the past 10 years as the Lord has been radically increasing my discernment. Since a child, I would discern things and just "know things" without any frame or reference to understand how or why I "knew things." As I grew and then met Jesus and walked with Him, I began to journey in understanding discernment; and believe me, I continue to learn and grow and certainly do not have all the answers, but I daily submit myself to His discipling of discernment in my life.

## Discerning God's Ways

It is imperative in these days that we are really allowing the Holy Spirit to disciple us in discernment, that we are arising as His daughters on earth discerning His ways and all that He is saying and doing. While also not being ignorant of the devil's schemes and being able to discern between good and evil and the discerning of spirits.

We are not to be conformed to this world, but transformed by the renewal of our minds, that by testing we may discern what is the will of God, what is good and acceptable and perfect (Romans 12:2).

As discussed at the start of this chapter, if we lack wisdom, we can ask God who gives generously without reproach and it will be given to us (James 1:5).

The call to ascend in discernment in this hour is crucial. First Corinthians 2:14 (ESV) says, "*The natural person does not accept the things of the Spirit of God, for they are folly to him, and he is not able to understand them because they are spiritually discerned.*" The Holy Spirit within us empowers us in our discernment and teaches us to not judge by appearances, but to judge with right judgment (John 7:24).

So in saying all of this, I believe the time has come, daughter. The time has come to make a decision to submit in greater ways to the Holy Spirit's teaching and leading in discipling you in discernment. The things He is going to reveal to you in these days and in the days to come are not only weapons placed in your hands, they are also gifts to guide you in His ways, His will, and His leading. And in these days, we need to walk in discernment more than ever before.

The time has come to make a decision to trust your discernment. The time has come to no longer have your head in the sand (if you have) trying to ignore the things He is showing you because you don't know what to do with it or it's hard to carry. Now is the time to truly *lean in* to what He is revealing. No more running and doubting what He is revealing, but rather leaning in and allowing Him to teach you.

Proverbs 2:3-6 (NLT) says, "*Cry out for insight, and ask for understanding. Search for them as you would for silver; seek them like hidden treasures. Then you will understand what it means to fear the Lord, and you will gain knowledge of God. For the Lord grants wisdom! From his mouth come knowledge and understanding.*"

I want to stop there for a second. The last part of that verse says, "*From his mouth come knowledge and understanding.*" He is the Source of our discernment. Knowledge and understanding come from the Lord. I believe in this hour that the Lord is calling us to really pay attention to our stewardship of discernment in a greater way. Part of that is definitely not doubting our discernment, but I believe the most important part of stewarding discernment in this hour is living deeply in the fear of the Lord.

## Discernment and Wisdom

We know Proverbs 9:10-12 says that the fear of the Lord is the beginning of wisdom. The stewardship of our discernment and divine intel He releases to us is fully dependent upon us walking in the fear of the Lord, recognizing *who* is speaking, revealing, and releasing discernment and wisdom to us.

That was a huge key that helped me in the place of doubting my discernment. It caused me to lean in closer and not be so quick to doubt what I was hearing and discerning. I wanted to worship the Lord with the stewardship of His discernment in my life, not doubt it. That brought me on my knees and on my face before Him to ask Him to help me to trust more than I doubt.

I have many times reflected on those words the Lord said to me and now I say to you, "*Do not doubt your discernment now or in the days ahead.*" I remember things that the Lord has spoken to me including, "*These are the days when you need My discernment more than ever before. With the rising deception and the dabbling in divination, it is imperative that you are living close to My heart and deep in My Word.*"

To arise as women of God fully alive in this hour, not doubting our discernment and walking fully armed with the discernment He is releasing, we must be daughters who are living close to His heart and deep in His Word. We cannot move from there. We must remain in Him and through Him. In His Word and through His Word. Nothing more, nothing less.

I tell you this, though—not doubting your discernment is not permission to move in pride or to be unteachable. It's a place of taking what you are hearing and discerning from the Lord and have a greater conversation with the Lord and as the Lord leads, with others whom you trust. Doubting our discernment causes us to flush our discernment and disregard it without further conversation. I feel the Lord's heart strongly that many daughters have been discerning things from the Lord, discerning the move of God and what the Lord is doing and/or wants to do, or discerning things of the enemy—but instead of continuing a further conversation with the Lord and/or with others, they disregard it. But the Lord is calling His daughters to not disregard their discernment in this hour.

Can I encourage you, do not jump quickly into the "trying to work it all out" box when discernment comes. Many times in my life I have jumped into that box and made assumptions or presumptions of what is going to happen, or how it's going to play out, or even at times made judgments when discernment has come. We really can't do that. We must avoid judgments, assumptions, presumptions and be continuously asking the Lord to give us wisdom and teach us how to walk out the discernment He is giving us in *His way* and with *His* heart.

## The Lord's Intel

The intel the Lord releases is never to be used as ammunition against another. It is not to be used as gossip or to parade intel or the secrets the Lord is releasing in discernment. This is far from the heart of the

Lord. The Lord is looking for those who will carry His discernment and intel with purity and integrity. As we carry His intel and discernment we *must* have His heart. We *must* be asking the Lord for His heart and what the assignment is with the discernment He is giving us. Often in my life if the Lord has given me discernment on something or revealed for example an issue in the body of Christ that He wants to purify or purge, I will not move or share *until* I have His heart.

*How* we carry discernment is so important, and asking the Lord to continue to teach us and allow Him to disciple us in discernment and carrying it is imperative in this hour.

As the Lord continues to disciple us in discernment, I hear the Lord's heart for you:

> *My daughters, I am arming you in this hour with the discernment that you will need for the days ahead. I am arming you and increasing your weaponry, and this weaponry is not to be reasoned out with natural eyes and with human logic. You* ***must*** *surrender and listen. You* ***must*** *humble yourselves and listen to what I am revealing. For this is a time when I am uncovering what is hidden in darkness. I am exposing the roots. I am exposing what has been hidden for many decades, even generations, and I am bringing forth what is impure into the light.*
>
> *I am bringing you higher into the place of seeing and discerning what I am speaking and what I am doing, and it requires a humble heart. It requires a heart that is humble, sensitive, and pliable to My Spirit. For I do not speak on human terms, nor do I speak on human agenda. I am speaking and revealing in this hour, bringing forth the hidden things both light and darkness. Do not doubt what I am speaking, My daughters.*

*For this is the hour when I am increasing your weaponry with discernment, and you must stay close to Me and deep in My Word to hear and discern what to do with what I am releasing.*

*Your voice is needed and I am increasing My roar from within you in this hour to intercede and to arise and speak. To be a voice, My voice on earth in every sphere of influence that I have given unto you. My daughters, there is a whole new realm of divine intel that I am calling you to step up into in this hour. Many of you have been living on the ground and from the ground, and you can live there no longer. You have been living under circumstances, lies, and muzzles, but I have been working deeply within your heart and within your life to cause you to arise on earth in a way you never have before.*

*Look around at the earth and look at how the kingdom of darkness is attempting to mar and break down My design; but, My daughters, listen to Me, I am raising you up for such a time as this, walking in your identity as My daughter, loved and adored by Me, gifted with My authority to not only see My Spirit move through you in power to tear down the kingdom of darkness, but to see My light and My glory shine through you like never before and see many come to know Me and My glory fill the earth.*

*You have doubted what you have discerned for too long. I am calling you to repent and to allow My Spirit to teach you in ways you have not yet known. I am inviting you deeper into a Jeremiah 33:3 space with Me to "call to Me and I will show you great and unsearchable things that you do not yet know."*

*I am calling you deeper into the chambers of My heart to* ***carry My secrets.*** *In this hour when I am dismantling structures and platforms within My Church where celebrity status has been elevated and trading floors have taken precedence, I am now bringing forth an army of men and women who walk in one accord discerning what I am saying and what I am doing and* ***not*** *being found to call evil good and good evil (Isaiah 5:20; Amos 5:15). It's time to be counted as one who will* ***stand for truth! My truth!***

I believe that fear has come against many daughters in so many ways to stop you from walking in the discernment God has given you. You have silenced the discernment because you haven't understood it or understood what to do with it. The Lord is now extending an invitation to you, to come and to be discipled—but there is a key positioning in this place of being discipled in discernment, it's humility.

To enter through this doorway of invitation into receiving greater divine intel in this hour and to walk in greater discernment, it is unto something. It's not unto you receiving intel for receiving intel's sake, it's for His plans on earth, His Kingdom being established like never before and His name being lifted high. To overturn the plans of the enemy and to partner with Him in all the glorious things that He is going to do on earth.

I hear the Lord saying,

*I am bringing you higher, My daughters, into a place of seeing and discerning what I am speaking and what I am doing, and it requires a heart that is humble, sensitive, and pliable to My Spirit. For I do not speak on human terms or agendas. I am speaking and revealing in this hour bringing forth the hidden things both light and darkness. For I am releasing divine intel in this hour not to be paraded and passed on. For I will deal strongly with those who take My divine intel and the whispers of My heart, and pass on this intel in whispers to others. I am looking for those I can trust with My intel and discernment in this hour. I am calling you, My daughters, deeper into the place of intercession. I am calling you deeper into the place of prayer. The divine intel and discernment I am releasing will call you deeper into prayer. I am strengthening you in these days and the days ahead in the discernment I am giving you, but do not use My divine intel or discernment and what I am revealing to you to gain the ears of others.*

## The Refiner's Fire

There is a refiner's fire coming upon hearts in this hour to prepare and purify us in greater ways as His army of daughters arising on earth with greater discernment. His refiner's fire is going to make room for the increase of His discernment in your life in this hour. As I have sat with the Lord, I can feel the urgency of His heart in this stewardship of purity in regard to His intel and discernment. Not everything He shares is to be shared. I'll say that again. *Not everything He shares is to be shared.*

One of the greatest tests in this season around the stewardship of discernment is when the Lord swears you to secrecy. I have heard the Lord say that when He shares His secrets in this hour, there will be times where He will swear you to secrecy, discernment, and revelation being given to you—as between friends. Think about this for a second, the King of kings and Lord of lords wants to share His heart and His secrets with you. The One who created the heavens and the earth is inviting you into a place of discernment to protect you, to guide you, to lead you, to position you, to use you, and to see His Spirit, His name, His light, and His love released through you on earth.

Think about this too. What would you say the goal of discernment is? If someone asked you that question, what would you say?

If someone was to ask me that question, I would say the goal of discernment is to know His heart, His will, and His *ways,* and to perceive and understand what He is speaking and revealing, His intentions. Discernment gives us the opportunity to continue to elevate His ways above all else and to partner with it. It uncovers and exposes what is not of God and shines the light upon what IS of God.

How truly blessed we are to have the Word of God that is a lamp for our feet and light to our path (Psalm 119:105) to help guide us, lead us, and teach us as we sit at His feet and listen to what He is saying.

I have mentioned this numerous times throughout this book that the Lord is moving us as His daughters and as the Church from defense to offense—and this is where deep divine insight and revelation, wisdom, and discernment is being released to you as you seek the Lord and sit deeply in His Word so you can partner with the strategies and plans of the Lord on earth.

You cannot expect to walk in increased discernment in this hour if you do not know the Word of God.

This journey of discernment and being discipled in discernment is not one to be done alone. It is not coincidence or accident that I continue to use the words "Army of Daughters" or "Company of Daughters" on earth, because you are not meant to walk this alone. You are not meant to journey this journey of being discipled in discernment alone. Absolutely the Lord is your Teacher and He is the

One who will disciple you and lead you and teach you, but there is safety, power, and wisdom found in community.

I have a few very close friends, that when the Lord allows me to share what I am discerning, what He is revealing and showing me, and I am really struggling with it, I will take it to one or two of these friends. They are safe spaces where there is loving, life-giving, and honoring conversations to pray and weigh the discernment that the Lord is releasing. These spaces have been life-giving for me. They are not places to "pass on intel," they are pure places where hearts are before the Lord to seek together what the Lord is saying and if what I am hearing or discerning is even of God. It's very important that we have these people and spaces in our lives when we are continuing to journey the journey of stewarding discernment and divine intel, especially in these days when discernment and divine intel is needed more than ever and the Lord is increasing our insight.

I hear the Lord saying, "***Do not dilute your discernment.***"

Daughters of God in the days ahead, do not dilute what God speaks to you and reveals to you. When these times come, you are going to carry His heart, His wisdom, and His tone to release and speak what He calls you to speak.

I hear Him saying:

> *As you marinate in the secret place in what I am speaking and revealing, as you spend time in My presence and knowing My heart and My Word, you will see My heart flow through what I call you to speak. In the speaking, I release this warning to you. My daughters,* ***be slow*** *to speak! Continue to cry out for wisdom as you release. Speak only when I call you to speak. Do not rush the release of revelation and discernment, for much of what I will show you is not for public view. You will see in the coming days more and more of an increase*

*in discernment and My divine intel for the hidden place of intercession. I am looking for those I can trust to carry My heart and My insight with purity, humility, and integrity. Do not doubt your discernment in this hour. As I speak, I will confirm. Remain in My Word. It's time to be discipled in discernment like never before.*

You can see, just in this chapter alone, how the Lord is continually repeating Himself. I know the Lord does that because He is trying to get our attention so His Word will take root within us and to highlight the importance of what He is speaking. The Lord speaks in repetition because He's so kind, He wants us to get it.

I don't want you to misinterpret the repetition and the urgency on the heart of the Lord for us to grow up into discernment and maturity in how to steward discernment and divine intel, as a place of fear. There are warnings and strategies that the Lord is giving us as He is calling us to come up higher and be discipled in discernment. He is giving us warnings to keep our mouths shut at times, to not rush revelation, to not doubt what He says, because He is raising up *you, me, us,* a company of women, who will stand for truth, who will not compromise truth, who will not dilute discernment, who will not back down, but will *remain steadfast.*

## Christ Alone

And in the days to come as the deception increases on earth, you will be called upon, daughter of God, to stand and to speak His truth and to discern what is of God and what is not. To see behind the veil and into the heart of matters where things are not what they seem in the natural and to truly see what's going on beneath the surface. To make declarations, to intercede, to pray, to stand and speak. To stand boldly on what He has revealed to you and shown you. The only way you can stand strong in the days ahead is to stand in *Christ alone.*

The hour is urgent, it doesn't take a prophet to see the hour is urgent. Darkness is increasing on earth, but we are not to fear the darkness, this is the Church's greatest opportunity to arise and shine (Isaiah 61) and to see the glory of the Lord fill the earth.

The fire upon your discernment, the call of the Lord that feels strong inviting you to truly live from your seat, to come up higher, the discipline and fire of the Lord upon doubt of discernment is not unkind of the Lord, it's the kindness of a loving Father preparing us for the days ahead. In the days ahead, you need to be strong in Christ, in your intimacy with Him, in making sure that as David says in Psalm 16:8 (TPT):

> *Because I set you, Yahweh, always close to me, my confidence will never be weakened, for I experience your wraparound presence every moment.*

Brian Simmons writes in his commentary notes:

> The Hebrew word *shava* carries the sense of being equal or similar. David was not saying he was equal to Yahweh, but that he thought the way God thought. David had made his heart and his mind to be identical with the art and mind of God. Always before himself, before anything, were the desires of God. It was the heart and mind of God that had first place in David's heart and thoughts.

Amazing isn't it? This verse has been burning in my spirit for so long in this season and as Brian summarizes it in this one sentence that follows, I believe is such a word for right now: "It is possible to translate this section as 'I have determined in my heart to be identical with the mind and heart of God and I will not let my resolve be weakened.'"

*Wow!*

Daughter of God, determine in your heart to be identical with the mind and heart of God and let not your resolve be weakened. We are going to look more into this in the next chapter, but this is such a key to being discipled in discernment in the days ahead. ***Determine*** to set the Lord ever before you and be identical with His mind and heart. As you stay in this place in the Word, at His feet, watch how He will disciple you deeper and deeper in discernment.

I hear the Lord saying, ***"Pay attention** to your discernment, do **not** doubt your discernment."* As the Lord is bringing things into the light, He is bringing with it, divine strategy in walking out what He is speaking. It is very important right now to pay attention to your discernment and to alignments and to where the Lord is leading. It is easy to get caught up in not understanding or trying to reason it out in the natural, but I felt the Lord strongly admonishing us, *"Do **not** doubt your discernment, follow My lead and strategy, for in that place I am leading you out of wrong alignments, leading you into new things I have for you and into new assignments before you."* And:

> *Lean in deeply and listen. I am calling you deeper into My Word and deeper into listening to My voice. For you cannot now give your ear to anything else but My voice. For in this hour it is imperative that you are following My voice wherever and however I lead you. You must be deep within My Word, for in My Word I am giving you divine insight and strategy that will accelerate you into a whole new level of wisdom, divine strategy, and discernment. For the enemy has come against many of you and told you that you are wrong,*

> *that you have heard wrong, you are in the wrong place, what you have seen is wrong, which has caused you to feel like you are living in a constant perpetual state of swirling confusion, but that confusion is being broken off in this hour and the assignment against your insight and clarity is being lifted off.* ***Remain*** *in My Word.*

You may have doubted your discernment for far too long. Those days are over. Accept the invitation to no longer doubt your discernment and allow Him to disciple you in greater ways, and in some ways you are about to see that you have been hearing and seeing right all along.

# 15

# DAUGHTER OF GOD, RAISE YOUR VOICE!

Daughter of God, powerful woman of the Lord, mighty warring woman of Zion (Psalm 68:11-12), I hear the Lord saying, *"Daughter of God, **raise your voice**."*

There is a call being released in the spirit from the heart of the Lord for you to *raise your voice* in this hour. It's not a raising of the voice in rebellion, it's not a raising of the voice to make noise, it's a raising of the voice of *authority*. There have been too many women in this hour who have been assaulted by the enemy's attacks and spirits of fear and intimidation that have come against you to silence you. But the Spirit of God has been moving powerfully and will continue to move powerfully in this hour to see the *sound* of His daughters arise on earth like never before.

I want you to hear this, precious sister, precious, powerful daughter of God, the enemy's time is up on restraining your voice any longer. The enemy is being evicted from the place of hindering your voice any longer. The Lion of Judah is roaring over you and breaking the chains that have contained your voice, it's time to *raise your voice*.

I have shared a lot in this book about boldness coming upon the daughters of God in ways we have never seen. The boldness of the Lord to stand and be a champion and agent of His truth, a warrior wielding the sword of the Spirit, the Word of God (Ephesians 6) and one whose voice is and will be used powerfully by the Lord to extend His Kingdom and tear down strongholds of the enemy.

I heard the Lord say, "My daughters, I want My river to flow from your mouths and your tongues to carry only My fire."

When the Lord spoke these words, two passages of Scripture came to my mind, Proverbs 18:21 and James 3:2-12.

Proverbs 18:21:

> *Death and life are in the power of the tongue, and those who love it and indulge it will eat its fruit and bear the consequences of their words* (AMP).
>
> *Your words are so powerful that they will kill or give life, and the talkative person will reap the consequences* (TPT).

James 3:2-12:

> *For we all stumble and sin in many ways. If anyone does not stumble in what he says [never saying the wrong thing], he is a perfect man [fully developed in character, without serious flaws], able to bridle his whole body and rein in his entire nature [taming his human faults and weaknesses]. Now if we put bits into the horses' mouths to make them obey us, we guide their whole body as well. And look at the ships. Even though they are so large and are driven by strong winds, they are still directed by a very small rudder wherever the impulse of the helmsman determines. In the same sense, the tongue is a small part of the body, and yet it boasts of great things.*
>
> *See [by comparison] how great a forest is set on fire by a small spark! And the tongue is [in a sense] a fire, the very world of injustice and unrighteousness; the tongue is set among our*

*members as that which contaminates the entire body, and sets on fire the course of our life [the cycle of man's existence], and is itself set on fire by hell (Gehenna). For every species of beasts and birds, of reptiles and sea creatures, is tamed and has been tamed by the human race.*

*But no one can tame the human tongue; it is a restless evil [undisciplined, unstable], full of deadly poison. With it we bless our Lord and Father, and with it we curse men, who have been made in the likeness of God. Out of the same mouth come both blessing and cursing. These things, my brothers, should not be this way [for we have a moral obligation to speak in a manner that reflects our fear of God and profound respect for His precepts]. Does a spring send out from the same opening both fresh and bitter water? Can a fig tree, my brothers, produce olives, or a grapevine produce figs? Nor can salt water produce fresh* (AMP).

*We all fail in many areas, but especially with our words. Yet if we're able to bridle the words we say we are powerful enough to control ourselves in every way, and that means our character is mature and fully developed. Horses have bits and bridles in their mouths so that we can control and guide their large body. And the same with mighty ships, though they are massive and driven by fierce winds, yet they are steered by a tiny rudder at the direction of the person at the helm.*

*And so the tongue is a small part of the body yet it carries great power! Just think of how a small flame can set a huge forest ablaze. And the tongue is a fire! It can be compared to the sum total of wickedness and is the most dangerous part of*

> *our human body. It corrupts the entire body and is a hellish flame! It releases a fire that can burn throughout the course of human existence.*
>
> *For every wild animal on earth including birds, creeping reptiles, and creatures of the sea and land have all been overpowered and tamed by humans, but the tongue is not able to be tamed. It's a fickle, unrestrained evil that spews out words full of toxic poison! We use our tongue to praise God our Father and then turn around and curse a person who was made in his very image! Out of the same mouth we pour out words of praise one minute and curses the next. My brothers and sisters, this should never be!*
>
> *Would you look for olives hanging on a fig tree or go to pick figs from a grapevine? Is it possible that fresh and bitter water can flow out of the same spring? So neither can a bitter spring produce fresh water* (TPT).

We see clearly here from Proverbs 18:21 and James 3:2-12 the exhortation of Scripture to watch our words and to use our words to bless, uplift, and speak life.

In multiple places in Scripture we see the principle of the mouth speaking as an overflow of what is in the heart.[5] I remember realizing the depth of revelation in this biblical truth, that the more I fill myself with His Word and His truth and meet Him in the Word and in the secret place, seeing His beauty, the more my heart is filled with the revelation of who He is and His truth. The more I see Him and the more I saturate myself in His goodness, the more my heart will overflow and testify of His truth and life—and the more I declare His truth and hear the Word of God, the more faith (Romans 10:17) would arise within me. That beautiful space of being saturated in His goodness and in His Word, oh how my heart overflowed and it was easy to speak and declare His truths and speak life.

## An Overflowing Heart

Then the valleys came, then the battles came, then the increased warfare seasons came, and guess what happened? Things that I didn't even realize were in my heart started to flow out of my mouth.

I then entered the "school of the mouth."

What do I mean by that? I wrote about this in my book *I Hear the Lord Say "New Era"*—an encounter about the new era that was to come, that we are now in, and that the Lord was inviting us into the school of the mouth. In 2019, I had an encounter with the Lord where He spoke over the decade of declaration, as He called it, "*Welcome to the school of the mouth.*" It was a beautiful invitation from the Lord to be schooled by Him in deeper ways in what comes out of our mouths, what we speak, which leads to a realm of revelation, of reintroduction to the power of our decree and the authority and power of the Word of God. I knew in that encounter that there was a weighty responsibility that was going to increase upon us in this new era to steward our words well.

Let me share with you an excerpt from the book:

> I heard the Lord say:
>
> *"Fire is coming upon the tongue and I am bringing major deliverance to My people of wrong declarations."*
>
> There is a major purification and conviction of the Holy Spirit coming into the body of Christ like we have never seen before to bring conviction and purification of words spoken.

For the Lord is going to bring forth deep healing in the hearts of many as they say yes to entering into the school of the mouth with the Lord. *"For out of the abundance of the heart the mouth speaks"* (Matthew 12:34).

The Lord is going to continue to convict and highlight words that are flowing out of the mouths of His people that are not in line with the Word of God and the truth of Scripture. It is the love of God that is going to bring the correction. He is going to the root of lies, unforgiveness, bitterness, and the place of "careless speech" as He trains His people in the power of words and the power in the tongue, because we are moving into a time when we will decree what the Lord is saying and there shall be sudden manifestation.

When the Lord spoke, *"Fire is coming upon the tongue,"* He spoke of conviction and purification, but He also spoke of commissions. This is the era when fire will fall upon tongues and a greater commissioning will take place of those being positioned to speak, sing, and declare the Word of the Lord. Many have lost their voice, and this is the era where voices will be restored. There is a mighty wave of His deliverance being released upon the tongue to deliver the people of God from declaring things that are not His heart, not what He is saying, and not His truth. God is dealing with lies and half-truths and leading His people into a place of declaring what He is saying and aligning with His Word.

I heard the Lord say, "Those who embrace the school of the mouth will have mouths that flow with heavenly wisdom that has never been seen before." (*I Hear the Lord Say, "New Era,"* p. 184)

Fire came upon my tongue and the conviction of the Spirit came upon me down to even the smallest things; the Lord was drawing me into a season of recognizing the power of my words and His Word and the importance of me speaking life. Oh how discouragement and weariness and lies of the enemy has filled my heart and were coming out of my mouth. But going through the school of the mouth—I continue to every day—awakened me in a greater way to what happens when we rehearse His rhema and we speak and decree the Word of God. I've heard it said many times that "the Kingdom is voice-activated," and indeed it is. Our hearts and mouths must be *full* of His Word, and we must speak only what He speaks.

Daughter of God, I feel such a roar in my spirit over your life. The enemy has tried too hard to keep you silent, he may have tormented you with his lies and stolen much from you and your voice. *This is the hour* of your restoration and your recompense. I see as you speak and declare in this hour, I see *miracles* manifesting. There is a recompense coming to you over the battle for your voice.

I see as you nestle deep into His heart and Word in this hour that the level of authority you are going to walk in is going to astound you. That authority has always been yours (Luke 10:19); and in this era, you are going to walk in it in ways you've never imagined. As you stay close to Him in the secret place and receive His counsel, He's working within you to bring you to another level of faith and demonstration of the power of His Word as you walk by faith, not by sight (2 Corinthians 5:7).

I see strongholds being demolished in this hour as you declare, as you pray, and as you stand upon the Word of God. This is truly the hour when God is releasing the roar of faith and His authority through your life to His Kingdom in greater ways to see a mighty advancing of the Kingdom take place and an occupying of territory that the Lord has assigned to you to take. There is also a mighty collecting of spoils that you will gather in this new era. There are spoils of war that you will gather and collect in Jesus's name.

Let's continue.

Isn't it interesting that in James 3:2-12 James talks about the power of the tongue and the second half of James 3:13-18 (AMP) talks about *wisdom*:

> Who among you is wise and intelligent? Let him by his good conduct show his [good] deeds with the gentleness and humility of true wisdom. But if you have bitter jealousy and selfish ambition in your hearts, do not be arrogant, and [as a result] be in defiance of the truth. This [superficial] wisdom is not that which comes down from above, but is earthly (secular), natural (unspiritual), even demonic. For where jealousy and selfish ambition exist, there is disorder [unrest, rebellion] and every evil thing and morally degrading practice. But the wisdom from above is first pure [morally and spiritually undefiled], then peace-loving [courteous, considerate], gentle, reasonable [and willing to listen], full of compassion and good fruits. It is unwavering, without [self-righteous] hypocrisy [and self-serving guile]. And the seed whose fruit is righteousness (spiritual maturity) is sown in peace by those who make peace [by actively encouraging goodwill between individuals].

Can you relate to how easy it is to be careless with your words, especially when you're tired? When you have been in a battle for so long and you're weary of contending? Or those seasons of intense warfare? My goodness, I have been there! Times when I have forgotten that my words create and words have just flowed out of my mouth that were not sowing seeds of life and truth, but words of death and discouragement.

I find these two portions of Scripture together in one chapter very interesting. We have here the call to tame our tongue and watch over our mouths and then in the second half of James chapter 3, a description on wisdom and the difference between earthly wisdom and heavenly wisdom.

As I look at the words the Lord spoke to me in 2019, I see the correlation: *"Those who embrace the school of the mouth will have mouths that flow with heavenly wisdom that has never been seen before."*

As we allow the Holy Spirit to deal with our hearts and our tongues and we posture ourselves in a place of deep humility and fear of the Lord and take responsibility over what we speak and what we allow to fill our hearts, treasuring His Words above all else, there will be mouths that will arise in this hour carrying the supernatural, pure, powerful wisdom of the Lord.

I have said this numerous times in this book, and I am going to say it again. God has been and will continue to raise up women of influence in this hour with the word of the Lord in their mouths. The warring women of Zion will declare the word of the gospel with power and deliver its message (Psalm 68:11-12)—the Esthers, the Deborahs, the Jaels in this hour with their mouths full of the wisdom of the Lord for such a time as this.

Daughter of God, recognize the power of your words and influence. Every step you take, everywhere you go, the Lord wants to use your mouth to release His wisdom, His life, His truth, and His prophetic voice.

It's all about surrendering to the process and training of the Lord to speak what He speaks and His Word and then see the manifestation of what He speaks come forth. I believe, daughter of God, that the Lord is raising up an army of mighty warring women in this hour who have swords in their mouths as we saw in Chapter 5.

I believe a woman of God who is living fully alive is a woman of God who has the river of God flowing from her mouth and is tending the garden of her heart before the Lord, allowing the Holy Spirit to examine and uproot any wicked way (Psalm 139:23-24). She is so in love with the Lord and His Word that she refuses to move from the Word of God until she sees the manifestation of what He has spoken (Isaiah 55:11). Is a woman of God one who gets it right all the time and is perfect? Nope, it's not about being perfect.

I believe a woman of God living fully alive is a woman whose heart is postured in purity before the Lord, wanting to worship God with her words. She is committed to watching over her heart and her words and placing the Word of the Lord at the highest place, and she is ever growing on her journey of recognizing the power of the Word of God in her life.

## A New Realm of Authority

The Lord is calling His daughters to raise their voices in truth, to raise their voices in prayer, and raise their voices in declaration. The Lord is raising up daughters with swords in their mouths. This is a new realm of authority that is flourishing in the hearts and lives of His warring women as they continue to come alive in greater ways to the revelation of who He is within them and that *His Word never fails.*

Disappointment and discouragement are not part of your story, daughter of God. The Lord is bringing you a new day of deeper awakening and revelation of *His Word never fails* (Luke 1:37).

It's time for the unrestrained voices of His daughters to arise; and listen to me, daughter of God, powerful woman of God, you are going to *demolish* strongholds of the enemy in this hour through what the Lord has you prophesy, has you pray, has you declare. Why have I spoken so much through this book about your voice? Because the enemy has come after your voice, he's come after your identity, he's come after your design and your destiny—*but those days are done.* The enemy has tried so hard to chase you out of your authority through fear, intimidation, comparison, and containment to silence your voice. Storms have tried to chase you away and sometimes have chased you away, but *hear* the word of the Lord to you.

I hear the Lord saying:

> *I am raising you up, My daughters, as* ***storm chasers.*** *Where storms have come and intimidated many of you and you have* ***run from*** *the storm, I am raising you up in this hour to* ***run toward*** *the storm in My authority and My wisdom and speak,* ***"Peace, be still."*** *There will be a greater overcoming of storms that you will see in this hour as you continue to arise in greater unprecedented revelation of your authority in Me and the boldness that you have not seen before, to take Me at My Word and not move until you see what My Word says come to pass.*

There is a mighty birthing of the Holy Spirit through His daughters in this hour; and as this birthing is taking place, a deep, deep deliverance from expectations that have been placed upon them of what their voice should look like and what it should sound like, is taking place. There is a mighty deliverance from fear and the fear of what others think—and a mighty awakening and activation of their *authentic* voices is taking place.

Let's stop there for a second, my friend, my sister in Christ, my fellow warrior in the Lord.

That is you. Your voice is powerful and your voice is needed. No one else has the same voice as you and that is exactly how it is meant to be. You are not meant to sound like someone else. The sound that is released through your voice in whatever form and shape that takes, is the sound that the Lord put inside you and the sound that the world needs to hear. It is the sound of His heart.

I want you to think of it like this for a moment. Your voice carries an expression and piece of His heart. Your voice carries a sound of His heart; and as that sound is released in all the places and areas God has called you to release it, that sound brings His manifest presence and the atmosphere of Heaven to earth. Then as your sound joins with the sound of another precious daughter of God, and another and another, think about the collective sound of His heart that resounds all around the earth. It releases the divine symphony of Heaven.

So whether your sound is loud and a roar, or your sound is gentle yet strong, all the sounds are needed. All together they play a part in releasing the melody of His heart and His Word and His justice, His love and His revelation that the world needs to hear. It's His voice through you that will lead many to Him. There is a strong, bold, unapologetic sound of the voices of His daughters arising in this hour. But hear me, friend, we are not all called to sound the same. So any insecurity, any comparison, any hiding, any shrinking back, any intimidation is being evicted in Jesus's name, as the Lord restores and increases your voice in this hour.

Years and years of women's voices being shut down or silenced are now being delivered and set free in accelerated ways, and a beautiful, humble confidence is being restored within many daughters of God and His voice through them.

## Arise and Fly

The Lord showed me that many precious daughters who had experienced having their voices shut down, for many different reasons, had broken and clipped wings. As the Lord was restoring their voices I saw their wings being healed. I then heard the Lord say, "*It is time to **arise and fly!** It is time to **arise and fly**.*"

The Lord showed me a huge waterfall of fire pouring over each precious daughter of God; and in some, it was igniting and increasing a roar and conviction within them that thundered, "I will no longer be silent." These beautiful daughters of God were being baptized in boldness. No longer shying away, they were arising in His boldness living *fully* alive in Him as they raise their voice at His leading.

It was then that I heard Him say:

> *Look at the unrestrained voices of My daughters arising up out of the wilderness, leaning upon Me. Look at their unrestrained voices. No longer contained by fear, insecurity, guilt, shame, condemnation, and the fear of others. Here they come arising up out of the wilderness like never before in this season, and they are being **called for**.*

I then heard the trumpet of the Lord and it was sounding *so* loudly. It was the call of the Lord as He gathered His daughters as a mighty army in this hour; the trumpet has sounded and they are being gathered, moving forward as that mighty army raising their voice at His leading and His voice through them would *break* the ground.

Daughter of God, your voice will break ground as you speak out what God has called you to speak, speaking forth with boldness and carrying His heart. As you speak forth what He calls you to speak, atmospheres are going to shift in ways you have never seen. As the Lord is raising you up in this hour, He is sending you forth into new assignments with an unrestrained voice—but you must stay close to His heart.

I hear the Lord saying, "*I am raising up My daughters in this hour and they are pioneering with their proclamation and praise.*"

Daughter of God, where the enemy has worked so hard to silence you on so many levels, there is a thundering of the Lord being released through your proclamation and your praise in this hour.

You may be reading this and your mind wanders to the journey that you have walked and how the battle over your voice was so intense that it almost took you out completely and you lost your voice. You may have stopped speaking out completely, others turned down the volume, others began to doubt the power of their voice or even if what they had to say made any sort of difference. Thoughts may have plagued you and assaulted you: "Someone else has already said that. No one listens anyway. Who am I to speak out?" Or, "I did speak out before but I got shut down." Or, "I spoke out what the Lord had me speak and the opposition that came against me was so intense because I didn't fit into a certain way of mold. So, I was rejected, shut down, and cast aside."

The battle over your voice has raged fiercely, and this is indeed the hour when God is going to pioneer through your proclamation and praise. God is taking you to a deeper level of understanding and revelation of the power that happens when you raise your voice and the power that happens when you proclaim His Word. His Word through you will break open the hardest ground and the hardest of hearts, bringing His Kingdom and His manifest presence, ushering in His love and His Kingdom culture and atmosphere.

He is going to break chains as you praise Him. Mighty deliverances are going to happen as you proclaim His Word. There will be such an increase in seeing bodies healed as you call bodies to come back into alignment, that by the stripes of Jesus they are healed (Isaiah 53:5). The Lord just showed me that many have fought much infirmity in their bodies and have been hit over and over by this spirit of infirmity—but in this season there are manifestations of healing that will come forth in the name of Jesus as you call *your* body back into alignment with the Word of God.

Watch in this hour of His power and His presence as He raises you up to release your voice, His heart and His sound through you, mighty shifts and moves of His Spirit will take place, *especially* through your intercession.

## Shake, Rattle, Roll

I hear the Lord saying that He is going to "shake, rattle, and roll" through your praise, proclamation, and intercession. Where the enemy has come and tried so hard to steamroll you and your voice, the Lord is raising *you* up in this hour to partner with Him in seeing His roar upon the declaration of His Word through you to shake, rattle, and roll the enemy's plans and demolish strongholds. He is releasing a roar through you in this hour that will cause the very plans of the enemy to be overturned. Whether your sound is loud or your sound is soft, there is a roar of conviction being birthed within you to *see* with your eyes what the Lord has declared in His Word.

Where the enemy has tried to dampen your flame, the Lord is deepening your flame in Him; and where the enemy has attempted to weaken your voice, the Lord is releasing His fire of conviction of the truth of His Word in our life being infallible. Remember, the Word of the Lord *never* fails.

I heard the Lord say, *"It's time to govern your world."* I felt so strongly that there are many who have been feeling like life and circumstances are steamrolling you. The areas where the enemy has tried to silence your voice is over your own life, your own heart, your identity, and your family.

The Lord showed me that it's time for you to turn the tables on the enemy and to raise your voice again. Yes, the Lord is raising you up in this hour to release your voice, release His hope, His love, His Word, His revelation, and His encouragement on earth, into your city, your nation—to be the voice He has called you to be. The Lord also wants you to govern your world in a greater way.

You, daughter of God, are called to live on the offense, not the defense. You are not called to live steamrolled by circumstances, emotions, fears, opposition, and concerns; you are called to live above that and in deep union with Him. I am in no way saying that you are not living deeply connected to Him, but I feel the Lord highlighting that there are some who will read this and have felt completely steamrolled the past few years, and maybe even longer.

The Lord showed me that you may have felt like you have forgotten what it feels like to live in victory. You are arising in greater strength to tell your soul to sit down and your spirit to stand up. You are arising in greater strength to tell the enemy and his accusations in your mind to be silenced with firm authority. The fire of conviction and authority will flow from your mouth saying, "That's not who I am." You will see many accusations no longer have a hold as you are renewed into His truth.

You are arising out of insecurity, the fear of what others think, comparison, and apathy into greater confidence in who He has created you to be and what you are called to release. You are arising to be comfortable in your own skin as you nestle into Him and His truth.

You are arising fierce in the revelation of your warrior King and His victory that sees the proclamation of what He is speaking and His decrees by faith met with greater power in this hour that sees signs, wonders, miracles, and the supernatural manifesting in the natural all around you.

You are arising, daughter of God, as one who no longer lives hiding or with a muzzled, constrained, or contained voice, or for some with no voice at all—you are arising with a bold confidence in the nature of the One whose voice flows from your lips, *His voice!*

It's time to raise your voice!

This is not your portion. That is not your inheritance in Christ. You have been through the fire, you have been through the hardship, you have been through intense warfare, but daughter of God, there has been a deep Refiner's fire to purge and purify. There may have been relentless opposition against you and you may be still facing it intensely, but the truth is, this is your hour to arise for such a time as this and know what it *truly* means to live deeply secured, anchored, and rooted in His love and identity. In Him you live completely secure in your authority and bold confidence in who He is in you and that He is for you.

I hear Him calling to the weary daughters of God and those who have felt like they have battled hard over their voice, "*Begin again.*" Arise and begin again. Take what He has spoken over your life and your family's life, take the promises of Scripture and begin to decree again. The Lord is calling you to arise more and more in this hour in the revelation that you are a gatekeeper. You are a gatekeeper of your heart and your eyes, you are a gatekeeper in your home (Proverbs 31), and you're a gatekeeper in all the areas of jurisdiction the Lord has given you through your proclamation, your decree, your intercession, and your praise.

## Turn the Tables

So let's go back to what I felt the Lord say, "*It's time for you to turn the tables on the enemy.*"

When I heard the Lord say this, the emphasis was very heavily upon the word *you*. It's time for *you* to turn the tables on the enemy. Daughter, friend, sister in Christ, it's time for you to arise and choose not to allow the enemy to steamroll you any longer. It's time to acknowledge again that the Word of God does not change according to your circumstances—the Word of God *changes you and your circumstances.*

Oh how the enemy has tried so hard to convince so many women that His Word will not come through for you, that His Word will weary you, or your prayers have become ineffective. But all of that is, what? *Lies!* Take a decisive stand against those lies and renew your mind (Romans 12:2) and know that God is restoring to you all that was stolen and lost. He is increasing and growing you up further into your authority and the revelation of our Mighty Avenger, our amazing God and His power and faithfulness.

It's time for fully alive women of God who have lost their voices to get them back. You are not raising your voice for raising your voice's sake, or even for you. You are raising your voice *for Him* and His glory and His Kingdom to be extended and for the generations.

Whether you have lost your voice or have found your voice, it's time to *raise* your voice and be bold to speak. It's time for you to be baptized afresh in the fire of conviction of the power of His Word and your *roar* is about to get louder than ever. *You,* daughter of God, sister in Christ, are taking back what is yours in Christ through your praise and proclamation.

You may have had spiritual laryngitis, feeling as if you've been speaking for so long but nothing much has shifted, so you lost or lowered your voice—*no more.* The Lord is restoring your strength and causing you to arise with new eyes. Be expecting in this season to experience deeper and deeper encounters with Jesus and the Spirit of wisdom and revelation in the knowledge of Him (Ephesians 1:17), which will activate, ignite, and increase the fire of conviction in you for the power of His Word to manifest in your life.

The Lord has been building endurance, maturity, and steadfastness within you through *all* you have walked—and now you are arising into a greater place of understanding by the Spirit of God and His wisdom, how to govern in greater ways with Him.

Woman of God fully alive, daughter of God with an unrestrained voice, *arise.*

The world needs your voice. The body of Christ needs your voice. Your family needs your voice. Your friends need your voice. We need to hear the voice that you have been created to hear, carry, and release—*His voice.*

As daughters of God, we will not be silenced. We will not be contained. We will not live in fear. We will arise as the unrestrained, unapologetic voices carrying the voice of our King, partnering with Him to see His Kingdom advance and strongholds shattered as the name of Jesus and His Word is declared through our mouths.

Daughter, it's a new day for you and for your voice!

# ENDNOTES

1 Brian and Candice Simmons, *The Sacred Journey: God's Relentless Pursuit of Our Affection* (The Passion Translation, Paperback)—A Heartfelt Translation of the Song of Songs,...Passion Translation Devotional Commentaries) (Broadstreet Pub Group Llc, 2015).

2 Based on Jennifer A. Miskov's website and her book, *Walking on Water: Experiencing a Life of Miracles, Courageous Faith and Union with God* (Silver to Gold, 2023), Chapters 4 and 6. Also see Miriam Huffman Rockness's *A Passion for the Impossible: The Life of Lilias Trotter* (2021).

3 Justin Allen; http://www.maidofheaven.com/foundation_joanofarc_please_god.asp.

4 Lana Vawser, *I Hear the Lord Say "New Era"* (Destiny Image Publishers, 2020).

5 Matthew 12:34, Luke 6:45 (AMP).

# ABOUT THE AUTHOR

Lana Vawser grew up in the Sutherland Shire, in NSW, Australia. She began her relationship with Christ in 1996, soon after which she started to understand and grow in her prophetic gifting both to individuals and the greater body of Christ. Since then she has ministered in various roles in local churches while posting prophetic messages through email lists or online. From 2014 Lana has been featured regularly on *The Elijah List, The Australian Prophetic Council,* and occasionally in *Charisma* magazine.

Lana Vawser has a heart to encourage the body of Christ and individuals in their walks with Jesus; deeper intimacy with Him; and learning to hear His voice. Lana operates in the prophetic and loves to share the heart of God with others. She has written several books including: *Desperately Deep—Developing Deep Devotion and Dialogue with Jesus; The Prophetic Voice of God; A Time to Selah;* and *I Hear the Lord Say "New Era."*

Lana is a gifted prophet and teacher and loves to see others grow in all that God has for them. She completed her Bachelor of Ministry through Tabor College in Sydney.

Lana and her husband, Kevin, live in Sydney with their four children.

Lana Vawser Ministries can be found online at lanavawser.com.

# In the Right Hands, This Book Will Change Lives!

Most of the people who need this message will not be looking for this book. To change their lives, you need to **put a copy of this book in their hands.**

Our ministry is constantly seeking methods to find the people who need this anointed message to change their lives. **Will you help us reach these people?**

**Extend this ministry by sowing three, five, ten, or *even more* books today and change people's lives for the better!** Your generosity will be part of catalyzing the Great Awakening that many have been prophesying and praying for.

From

# Lana Vawser

**Embark on a wild and unique prophetic adventure with God!**

The New Testament makes prophecy a priority for *all* believers: if you are indwelt by the Holy Spirit, you are called to hear God's prophetic voice!

But if this is true, why do so many believers struggle to receive God's voice in this way?

Lana Vawser empowers you to hear God for yourself by tuning in to how He is uniquely speaking to you!

Through easy-to-understand, revelatory teaching and powerful stories, Lana illustrates how God has created all believers to hear His voice in their own distinct way.

Tune in, and receive your word from the Lord!

**Purchase your copy wherever books are sold**